her voice

the curated wisdom of brilliant women

LOUISE ATKINSON

For my grandma, Cath. The strongest woman I know.

Copyright © 2024 by Louise Atkinson.

All rights reserved.

No part of this book may be reproduced or distributed in any form without prior written permission from the author, with the exception of non-commercial uses permitted by copyright law. No part of this book may be reproduced or transmitted by any means, except as permitted by UK copyright law or the author.

Cover illustration by Naim Solis.

MOJA PUBLISHING

Contents

Introduction

Part 1 – Self

1. The system was built without women	2
2. Unpack your baggage	10
3. Put yourself first	17
4. Give yourself time and space to heal	26
5. Pursue your purpose	34
6. Connect deeply with yourself	40
7. Childbirth is not 'routine'	48
8. Sharing your pain can help others	54

Part 2 – Work

9. Times have changed ... kind of	62
10. Reach for your inner confidence	68
11. Know your own strength	76
12. It's not you, it's them	82
13. Be where you can thrive	88
14. The motherhood penalty	96
15. Find a balance that works for you	104
16. When your worlds collide	111

Part 3 – Community

17. The war on women	117
18. The cultural context	128
19. Resist the pressure to conform	137
20. Don't let anything hold you back	143
21. Think free	152
22. Pick your partner with care	157
23. Be part of the support crew	165
24. The next generation	175

Epilogue
Resources
Acknowledgements
About the author

Introduction

The kitchen table

When I was a little girl, I would go to my grandparents' house most days. Their small bungalow in Hull was the central hub of our family. When I go back there now, which I don't very often, the comforting smell of the house takes me back to the days and weeks and years I spent growing up there.

My fondest memories are of being there for Sunday lunch. My grandad and uncles would tinker in the garage or the garden, talking about work and their hobbies. My grandma would be cooking in the kitchen, and all the women would be there too, sitting at the table with a pot of tea or helping with the cooking. They would talk about everything – the baby still isn't sleeping through the night, my son is getting into trouble at school, my husband is quiet and I think he's worrying about money.

Across the generations, they had a common perspective from which to share the wisdom that had been passed down through the generations of women before them. At the kitchen table, they taught each other to mend clothes, shared home remedies for period pain, and provided a safe ear for each other. Sometimes they provided moral support. Sometimes they argued. Sometimes they just gossiped and had fun! But the lessons of their own mothers and grandmothers came through in their conversations – their shared experiences bonding them through the generations.

Throughout history women have come together to form support networks, and this didn't just happen within families. Women shared their wisdom over garden fences, at social groups, at church, down the bingo – everywhere. Women in lace-making factories, fishwives in fish markets, mums at home with babies... all the way back to when humans lived in caves, we have bonded over a common sense of purpose, and we have lived our lives together.

Today, my kitchen table is a place for snatched breakfasts on the way out of the door and, if we're lucky, a family dinner a few nights a week. Our society has changed so much, and women have lost the places where we could seek the wisdom of other women. We no longer live on the street where we grew up, with our extended family; we no longer play a key role in raising each other's children and supporting each other.

Like a lot of women my age, I am the first in my family to have a career and work full-time as well as being a wife and mother. I can't go back home and sit at my mum's kitchen table and talk to her about how to manage my new promotion within the rigid childcare I can afford, or how to handle the difficult person at work who keeps undermining me. Our worlds have drifted apart.

But, worse than this, the information we do have access to has huge gaps in it, and we can't even see them. From medical research to product design, the world is not made for women. Even something as accepted as the 9–5 working day was designed for men with wives at home! The correct dosage of heart medication, the "safe" width of a seatbelt, the symptoms of ADHD, and millions of other things, have been developed from thinking that excludes women.

And the truth is, women are different to men. We are biologically different. The social constructs that we live within are different. The implications and consequences of things that happen to us are different.

So, if we don't have access to generational wisdom, and conventional "truths" are tainted by a biased system, where do we go for support? We might feel lost, trying to navigate this brave new post-feminist world, surrounded by Instagram posts of perfect mothers with their perfect children, and tropes about smashing the patriarchy. I know many women who are so caught up in trying to be everything to everyone, they have forgotten who they are.

I don't want this for my daughter. She's thirteen, and she's a force to be reckoned with. She's smart, strong and funny. Unlike most girls her age across the world, she has a million opportunities at her feet. And I want her to walk into the world having access to the sort of wisdom, passed from incredible women, that our mothers and grandmothers had.

This wisdom is being cultivated by this generation of women, every day. The transition team.

The women balancing motherhood with a demanding career, becoming the *firsts* – the first female MD or CEO in their company, the first female speaker at the medical conference, the first woman in their family to graduate from university. The women living their lives, doing amazing things, raising their families, changing the world one day at a time, and doing it quietly and without fanfare.

I am very lucky to be surrounded by these women. I work with them. They are my friends. They are my fellow mums at the school gate. I learn from them every day, even when they don't know they're helping me. Through testing times in my own life, I have come to realise that, through these brilliant women, I have access to a library of insight.

I started talking to the women in my life in more depth, and they told me the most amazing stories – experiences that had shaped their lives and approach to the world. They talked to me about how they saw themselves, and what had happened to influence this. They talked about their experiences at work, and how they were navigating the huge changes in the workplace. We talked about the communities we live in, and our relationships with other people.

With their permission, I started writing their stories down, because I knew other women would find them as inspiring as I did. I called this work Project Sunlight, because, like sunlight, my time with these women renewed me, inspired me, and helped me to grow.

I became curious about the themes that emerged through our conversations. I read books, reports and academic papers. I found a world of information that put these stories into context and gave me an insight I didn't have before.

I started reaching outside my network, and I met the most incredible women. Some were friends of friends, some were women I knew through my professional network –

I even spoke to women on the train! The stories they so generously shared felt like beautiful gifts. They are told here, as closely as possible, in their own words. Some have been given anonymously, and I have worked with the women to change details to protect their privacy or the privacy of others. These are their personal accounts.

It's time to fill the gap that was left when we got up and walked away from our mothers' kitchen tables to explore the freedoms feminism has afforded us. It's time for us to share the new wisdom we have learned with the next generation of women and girls, and with each other.

Part 1 – Self

Chapter One

The system was built without women

Nia is a forty-nine-year-old mother of two. She lives in Glasgow with her husband and children and is a physiotherapist specialising in sports injury rehabilitation.

"*I never thought it would come to this. All my life I've been the picture of health – sporty at school, I was captain of the hockey and netball teams, and I dominated at cross-country running. I even beat the boys! I kept up my love of sport through to adulthood, running regularly, going to the gym, and playing team sports wherever I could. My job meant I lived in sportswear and was always surrounded by sportspeople. It was where I felt most myself. I was lucky to recover quite easily from both my pregnancies, and by forty I was still feeling great.*

But not long after my fortieth birthday, I started feeling fatigued. It swept over me, and some weeks it never seemed to go away. At first, I chalked it up to stress – working long hours, not getting enough sleep and running around after the kids. But then I started suffering from muscle pain, constant headaches and a general sense of heaviness that hung over me like a dark cloud. Some days I couldn't even describe it, but I just didn't feel well, and people started to comment on it. I developed a rash on my scalp and on the tops of my ears, and patches of discolouration on my skin. As a Black woman, this was really noticeable on my arms and legs, and nothing I did seemed to help. Eventually I went to see my doctor. After a few tests, he told me it was nothing serious: 'Just stress', he said. He gave me some basic lifestyle advice and sent me away. I wanted him to be right so I tried to push through it, hoping if I just got more rest I'd be OK.

Months passed and my symptoms got worse. I began to experience chest pain and shortness of breath. My heart would race and I suffered terrible dizzy spells – sometimes at scary times like when I was driving. I went back to my doctor, insisting that something was wrong. He ordered more tests but found nothing: 'Your tests are normal – maybe it's anxiety. Have you considered seeing a therapist?' I didn't know what else to do, so I reluctantly agreed.

I saw a therapist for six weeks. She was kind and patient but despite our regular sessions, my symptoms were not improving. The crushing fatigue and dizziness were getting in the way of me doing the things I loved, stopping me living my life. I started to feel like I was crazy, that it was all in my head. My friends and family began to look at me with pity or frustration when I had to cancel plans or leave a playdate with the kids half an hour after arriving; they wondered why I couldn't just snap out of it. My husband was supportive, but I felt guilty for placing the extra burden on him when I couldn't get the kids to school or make dinner and he had to cancel work plans to do it while I stayed in bed.

One evening, I came across an online forum for women with undiagnosed health issues. When I read their stories, they felt very familiar. I read stories about women struggling to get a diagnosis of heart disease or endometriosis, and a couple of stories about a condition called lupus. I had heard of lupus but knew nothing about it. The symptoms the women described were almost identical to mine. As I researched the condition, I learned that African American women are three times more likely to develop lupus than white women, that it's more severe and tends to develop at a younger age. Armed with this information, I went back to my GP practice – and I asked to see a different doctor.

Based on the information I had gathered, I asked to be referred to an autoimmune specialist. From there, I met Dr Patel, who ordered a series of tests that hadn't been done before. A week later, I got a call while I was on my way to drop the kids off at school.

'You have lupus,' he said gently. I took the kids into school, said goodbye, got back in my car and cried my eyes out. Relief, mixed with anger and frustration, washed over me. For nearly a year I had been misdiagnosed and dismissed. Dr Patel explained that lupus is often overlooked because it doesn't follow the 'textbook' symptoms in women – and particularly women of colour – that doctors are trained to recognise.

Treatment started immediately. Although I had a long journey before I'd feel like myself again, I finally knew what I was fighting. Looking back, I wish I had listened to my intuition and pushed sooner for the right help. No one knows your body like you do. Sometimes you need to fight to find the right person: one who can see you as a whole person, not just a list of symptoms in a textbook."

Did you know that every single cell in our body has a sex? From our skin cells to our heart cells, at a cellular and biological level we are female. We have different hormonal patterns to men, we grow hair in different places, our fat distribution is different. In fact, we are so different that you can tell men and women apart simply by looking at them. Women can grow and birth another human being and grow body parts inside us that we don't even have ourselves! Our bodies work differently to men's bodies and respond differently to things. Obvious, right?

Well, no.

Even in 2024, we simply know less about female biology than about male biology. For 200 years, Western medicine has largely excluded women from scientific work. Female health has been underresearched, misconstrued, and twisted to fit a male agenda. Apart from in reproductive medicine, male biology has largely formed the evidence base for the diagnosis and treatment of both men and women.

Throughout history, most doctors, researchers and scientists have been men, and as recently as twenty-five years ago, most US college boards representing medical specialties across the world were almost exclusively male. Perhaps this explains why erectile dysfunction, which affects 19 per cent of men, is studied five times more often than premenstrual syndrome (PMS), which affects 90 per cent of women.[1]

Most of the cells, animal and human, studied in medical science have been male. This isn't an accident: in fact, for many years it was a matter of policy. In 1977, following the thalidomide scandal, the US Food and Drug Administration (FDA) recommended that all women 'of childbearing age' – so basically from late teens to mid-fifties – should be excluded from all clinical research.[2] The intent was to protect any potential unborn children from unforeseen side effects, but it applied whether or not women were in relationships or considering having a baby. This wasn't reversed until 1993. Unsurprising, then, that drugs approved based on male-only research have a significantly higher risk of side effects in women. The picture is even more stark for women of colour, who are still significantly underrepresented in clinical research.

This has catastrophic effects for women, how we are treated, and the sorts of treatment we are offered. As Maya Dusenbery highlights in her brilliant book, *Doing Harm*, for many conditions (including Parkinson's disease, irritable bowel syndrome (IBS), coronary artery disease, neck pain and tuberculosis), men are offered more extensive investigations and treatments than women when they present with the same symptoms. Older women are less likely than older men to be admitted to intensive care units or to receive lifesaving interventions.[3] When they present with pain, a man is more likely to receive painkillers; a woman is more likely to receive sedatives.[4] Women are more likely to become disabled after a stroke.[5] We wait longer to be diagnosed with cancer.[6]

The impact of this is not just medical but also psychological. Women have more negative experiences when trying to get help for our health. We are questioned, judged, rejected, ignored. Women have to work harder to attract a doctor's attention, to be believed and taken seriously.[7]

The purpose of setting all this out is not to scare anyone – and it's certainly not to denigrate the health service or health professionals. In the UK, we are so lucky to have the NHS and the people who work within it. Our medics work incredibly hard and are bright, caring people. This isn't about that.

But knowing this means we can take control of our own health. The medical services we receive are not perfect. They are not perfectly resourced and they are not based on perfect information. It means we know where we stand and can take a different approach.

If the healthcare system is not helping you, maybe your doctor is responding to you based on bias. Maybe they are responding based on inaccurate or incomplete information. Maybe both, maybe neither. But only you are accountable for your own health. Own it. Do the research. If you think you are not being listened to, quieten that voice in your head that's telling you to stop complaining and push to be heard.

1. *Independent:* (Article, 2016) Erectile dysfunction studies outnumber PMS research by five to one.

2. Association of American Medical Colleges: (Article, March 2024) Why we know so little about women's health.

3. National Library of Medicine: (Study, December 2007) Sex matters: gender disparities in quality and outcomes of care.

4. Harvard Medical School: (Article, October 2017) Women and pain: Disparities in experience and treatment.

5. Centre for Women's Health: (Article, 2019) In stroke, outcomes differ for men and women.

6. National Library of Medicine: (Study, 2016) Large-scale characterisation of gender differences in diagnosis prevalence and time to diagnosis.

7. *Social Science and Medicine:* (Journal, 2003) It is hard work behaving as a credible patient: encounters between women with chronic pain and their doctors.

Chapter Two

Unpack your baggage

Anna lives in London with her family. She works as a coach and wellbeing consultant.

"When I was five years old, my mother sat me down and told me, in a very matter-of-fact way, that my father was going to die in six months. She told me how it was: this is how long he has to live and we have to be strong. Don't cry. It is what it is.

He went on to live for another fifteen years.

I went into his room every morning to check he was still alive. My mum dealt with all of this like it was normal – or at least, that's how it seemed. She had a good career as a headteacher and was fiercely independent, but she struggled to deal with her emotions. She came from a family where there was no place for emotions or being weak. That's how my grandparents would have defined resilience.

I had a misunderstanding about resilience for a long time because of that. I was asked to be strong, not complain, get on with it, and told that what doesn't kill you makes you stronger. I strongly believed that was the case, until I decided it wasn't – and there was an important trigger in my life that helped me see this.

I was working in sales in a very tough environment. The definition of "performance" was what you delivered each month. You were only as good as your last month, and everyone told you that openly – there was no sugar coating! I ended up in sales by chance and was highly ambitious and driven. If I wasn't in the top five for the company, I saw it as a failure – and I thought that was healthy. My performance at work was what I was being rewarded and praised for. The environment was reinforcing my belief that performance was about the number, and of course this is true: companies exist to make a profit. But, at the time, I thought "performance" meant not complaining and staying strong and resilient, whatever happened. It served me well and the company rewarded me for it.

I took over an office that had been without a manager for quite a while. I was put into the role with no management *training, and no team, as most people had left due to stress. I thought, 'What's wrong with them?' I remember saying to my boss (a woman): 'It is what it is. I don't know why people complain.' She loved that and would hold me up to the others and say, 'Look at Anna – she just says, "it is what it is" and never complains.' I got her a gift, a framed print saying 'It is what it is' and she put it in a prominent place in her kitchen. She thought that was the attitude everyone should have; the mindset was reinforced again.*

She was the only female director in the company, and there were only three female sales managers, out of about eighty. I behaved like her a lot of the time – you had to be that person to be heard. If you approached a situation with empathy and understanding, you had no place there. We had to behave like this. If we didn't, we'd never get promoted, that's for sure.

Unfortunately, this wasn't sustainable. I ran an office that was supposed to be staffed by a team of five on my own, sometimes with one other person. While I didn't complain about it, unsurprisingly it started to affect my health. I started waking up in the morning and thinking 'I can't do this anymore. I just can't.' But I had all these beliefs from childhood telling me 'What doesn't kill you makes you stronger' and 'Just keep going, it will be fine'. The combination of these beliefs and a toxic work environment reinforcing these beliefs got me to the point where I just couldn't do it anymore.

The day things changed was the day my boss went on maternity leave. My husband, who could see the toll work was taking on me, told me, 'It's just not worth it. Yes, we need the money but you need your health more. Either they get you some help or you quit.'

I called my boss and I told her I needed some help, as I couldn't cope any more. She said she was sorry, there was nothing she could do and that I was doing a great job. I told her, in that case, I resign. Understandably, she reacted badly to this, saying that I couldn't do this to her. In the end, I agreed to work my notice and she went on maternity leave.

A new director took over, and with him I had what was probably the most important conversation of my professional life. He said he respected my decision to leave but wanted me to stay, and asked what the company could do to keep me, including allowing me to work in a different department. He asked me to take the rest of the day off and think about it and said he would give me any support I needed.

And that's exactly what he did – he gave me the support I needed (a full-time administrator and eventually a couple of negotiators), and we talked most days. He asked me how I was doing and if there was anything I needed. It was a very different approach to management! I stayed and I ran the office for two more years after that.

For a long time afterwards, it was like I had PTSD (post-traumatic stress disorder). It was such a traumatic experience, and I almost felt like a victim. But looking back a few years later, I think it was actually caused by my lack of self-awareness and a lack of flexibility in my thinking about what resilience meant. I had an unrealistic expectation of myself. It wasn't my boss's fault – she was a very good leader in many ways. She had just been promoted into that role, and there were very high expectations of her too. She's not a bad person. I like her, and she's still doing a great job for the company. We are all shaped by our relationships and the environments we have been part of. Some people are not very self-aware and I am a perfect example of that. I defined resilience the way I did because it helped me survive a horrible situation as a child.

But as I built my own self-awareness, I developed a much greater understanding of my own behaviour and that of other people, and it was this that guided my career choice and led me to what I now do professionally. After leaving this role, I transitioned to working in learning and development, and studying coaching and behavioural change science – the science of human behaviour and motivation. I pursued a career as a coach and wellbeing consultant, which involves listening to people's stories and helping them develop greater self-awareness, and attitudes and behaviours that support resilience, wellbeing and sustainable performance at work."

Everyone has baggage. The experiences that make up our lives, both good and bad, affect not just how we behave, but also how we see the world. They affect how we see ourselves. Things that look like choices can be behaviour that is deeply ingrained in our psyche. The behaviour that Anna considered to be positive for her life was the very thing that was hurting her.

The same applies to the people around us. They are working out their own stuff, and usually doing the best they can. It's rare to find people who are deliberately out to make our lives worse, although they do crop up from time to time. Through a lot of reflection, Anna was able to see that the woman putting her under so much pressure was simply dealing with her own baggage too.

The dangerous thing about baggage is that we can't always see it. It can take real work to get to the bottom of what's driving unhelpful behaviour, both in ourselves and others. Often, this work comes at a time that is out of your control, or at a crisis point, and then it's forced upon us.

Wouldn't it be better if we could reflect on what's hurting us throughout our lives and make small changes along the way, rather than waiting for something to go wrong? Because life is so busy, it can be impossible to find the time to reflect on our behaviour and our choices, and consider what might be driving us, and whether that's positive or negative.

A lot of people have an anecdote from their youth that plays an important role in their psyche – it's usually something a teacher said to them or a name they were called by other kids at school, or a bad experience with an early relationship. Sometimes these experiences are big, traumatic things, like Anna's childhood experience. But even seemingly small things can have a huge impact on how we interact with the world and the choices we make. Making the effort to understand what we're carrying around with us, and whether it is truly serving us well, can have a massive impact on our lives and our happiness. In Anna's case, a simple conversation with her boss turned a situation that was breaking her into one that supported her success. It set her on a course to a new career, where she can help others achieve the same level of self-awareness that was so important for her life.

Chapter Three

Put yourself first

Lindsey is a forty-eight-year-old woman who lives in Mansfield with her husband Paul, their eight-year-old son and their cat. She works in the public sector implementing supplier relationship management.

"*My mum has been, and always will be, my best mate. She always wanted me to know that no matter what, I could go to her. She would rather know the bare honest truth even if she didn't like it. She wanted to be there for me in my darkest times as well as my best. My friends at school would all be telling little white lies about where they were going, saying they were going to the cinema when actually they were off clubbing. My mum was the one dropping me off at the door and picking me up at 2 a.m. That was my mum! She wanted me to have a safe space with her, rather than having me lie to her and as a result I never did. She had a difficult childhood herself and wanted to be the opposite of everything she had experienced in her younger years. We, her family, were her world.*

In 2017 Mum got diagnosed with dementia. In reality, it had gone on for several years before then. The telltale signs had been there, and her behaviours gradually changed. When she was formally diagnosed, she wouldn't accept it – she was in denial. As is the case with dementia, paranoia was a common occurrence for Mum in the early stages. Everybody was in a conspiracy against her, even the doctors. It was really hard to deal with.

At around the same time, I had my son Lewis. Becoming a mum for the first time is such a huge thing. I'd been very career driven until then and building my own family was amazing. Lewis was only six months old when Mum was diagnosed. I had always had the picture-perfect idea in my head of what it would be like when my mum could not only be the most amazing mum, but finally have her moment to be the most amazing grandma too. She would have spoilt him rotten, and he would have had her wrapped around his little finger. She would have adored and cherished him the way she did all her family. When you're pregnant, you build this picture in your mind of what it's all going to look like; our relationship evolving into a whole different level that we would experience together as a mother and grandmother. And that never came to be.

The irony of it was, and it almost happened in tandem, as Lewis was developing new skills, whether that be walking, talking, being independent and eating on his own, my mum was doing the reverse. Our beautiful friendship that I just instinctively thought would always be there was deteriorating at the same pace. It was really hard and really draining. Alongside all the joys of becoming parents for the first time and wanting to cherish every minute of that, I also became the accountable person for all the horrific things you have to navigate with dementia.

My dad came from a family that didn't show emotion. Powering through was their way but also meant sticking his head in the sand to our deteriorating reality with Mum. I found myself not only dealing with the emotions of Mum's regression but also taking the lead on all the proactive stuff needed to understand how to deal with dementia – navigating what felt like a complex world of social care, hospitals, doctors and mental health. Mum and Dad had lived a normal life – he was the "breadwinner" and proud of his career and whilst Mum had a successful career for many years as a designer and manager, she did the lion's share of raising three kids. They had dreamed of their retirement, spending six months abroad in a caravan through winter in the UK and then coming back. He had delayed retirement because of the purpose he felt from his work, which is now the biggest regret of his life. He lost valuable and precious time with Mum as they only had twelve months when he finally retired before dementia changed it all for them. When we reached out for support for my parents, we were often sent in circles within the care system. We were told we were 'coping too well' and that Dad needed to be on the brink for our voices to be heard. So I continued to be his core support.

When I went back to work after having Lewis, I negotiated a four-day compressed week, and when Lewis started nursery, I kept my Fridays off so I could care for my mum and provide a day of respite for my dad. There were tasks that my mum only trusted me with. My Fridays were often spent with a bowl of water, stripping her down and cleaning her. We tried to bring carers in, but she wouldn't let them bathe her – when they tried, she became very aggressive. She once spent eleven weeks in the same clothes as we were asked to step aside and resist intervening whilst they tested if home care could work three times a day. It didn't. So Dad and I would spend Fridays getting her clean and fresh before he took some well needed time to shop and take some time for himself. It was a heartbreaking phase of her condition but when you love someone you just do it.

And through all this, I didn't miss a beat at work. Only once did I miss a Teams call. My mum called me frantically – Dad had gone to the shop and, when he had come back, she didn't know *who he was and had locked him out. She wouldn't let him in, was petrified and had called the police. They had heard her threatening his life so couldn't leave the situation until I went and helped her calm down. I phoned my boss and explained I needed to be away for half an hour. Despite my personal challenges, I was working hard, travelling a lot, delivering my best and making a difference for my business.*

When my year-end review came around, my boss gave me feedback that if I wanted to continue to progress my career, I was going to have to come back five days a week. He said, 'You can't continue this four-days-a-week behaviour, people will just become aggrieved by that.' As shocking as it was looking back at it (it was just one of a string of inappropriate and unacceptable experiences with this manager), at the time I just sat there and thought, well, the inevitable will come, my mum will pass soon and when she does, I'll think about it.

Mum is in care now, and she's in the final stages. She has no idea who we are, and she can't do much at all for herself anymore. It's tough – they call dementia the long goodbye and it's absolutely true. Typically, when you lose somebody, you mourn them and grieve them and the loss of them physically gives a degree of closure to enable you to move forward and find ways to cope. Clearly, every loss is painful no matter, but with this we have no closure as yet. Mum is still dying in front of my eyes every day and the essence of who she was has disappeared. You never know your last moments of something, and each brings a new kind of pain – she's forgotten my name, she's forgotten my face, she can't speak, she's incontinent. It's constant heartbreak.

I'm living this journey whilst still trying to be the perfect mum and make the most of all the amazing memories that go so quickly when you've got a little one, and be a great partner, and progress my career and be there for my team; show up, smile and be positive. I remember my dad making this comment – he made it with all good intent – that I was now the matriarch of the family and had picked up where Mum had left off. Without realising it, the pressure he put on me to step in and be the matriarch was stifling. I didn't want to be the matriarch. I didn't want to step into those shoes. I wanted to be me.

I was lucky to be able to see a therapist through work. I wanted to talk to someone who wasn't connected to me and didn't really know me. She helped me see that, to the outside world, I was handling life incredibly well – almost too well – but my self-care was terrible. I had become a lynchpin, and the problem with being a lynchpin is that, if you crumble, everything around you crumbles too. An amazing colleague gave me some really simple advice – categorise your stuff into needs, wants and shoulds, and just observe how much you do because you think you should, compared to the things you truly want and need. I started to test my decision making and the choices I made with those principles in mind. Am I meeting that person for coffee because I feel obligated to? Am

I doing something because I think that's what a good mum looks like rather than what I need in that moment? My life was ridiculously off balance with so many "shoulds" that I didn't make space for any needs or wants. When I did, I felt guilty for it. I'd feel bad for having my hair done once every twelve weeks because that was time away from our family. I've had to learn to enable the self-care and allow myself to do things that I need. I'm entitled to. It's okay.

I now give myself permission to weed out thoughts and environments that are negative and toxic. You're allowed to feel how you feel. You're allowed to be tired. You're allowed to be weak. You're allowed to be sad. You don't have to be this powerhouse of strength continually. It's still a work in progress but my wellbeing matters, and I am conscious of it now. Walking my path of dementia gives me a constant and piercing perspective that I try to never lose sight of."

Women have the most immense capacity. We can be many things all at once and cram it all into a seven-day week! The cliché of women being able to multitask is truer these days than ever before. But so many women I know put themselves at the bottom of their own priority list. We are the givers of everything, to everyone, all the time. This dangerous narrative of sacrifice has eroded the most basic elements of our lives to the point where we feel guilty for just trying to meet our own basic needs. "Self-care" is packaged as a selfish treat we indulge in once everyone else's needs are taken care of. God forbid we might need a walk or a nap or a coffee with a friend. We spend so much time and effort focusing on our kids getting their five-a-day and going to bed on time. We fill their lives with enriching activities and refill their water bottles. But then we survive on takeaway coffee and eat on the go, running from work to school pick-up to navigating a hundred after school clubs. Day after day. Week after week. For many women, their own wellbeing comes last, because the standards we are being held to, sometimes by ourselves, are unachievable and unrealistic.

Sadly, it seems to have become a badge of honour – a competition about who is busier. There's comfort in sharing our pressure with others, but let's not reinforce that it's normal. Let's not set the bar so high for ourselves and each other that there is shame attached to taking some rest. If we see rest as a luxury, rather than a necessity, we will never get enough. We will end up in survival mode, just trying to get through the next day, week, school term, financial year, reserving our rest time for holidays. And then we break.

We weren't supposed to live like this. We need downtime to think, reflect and explore our thoughts. Rest gives us perspective and allows us to open up the more creative parts of our minds. We need rest for both our physical and mental wellbeing, and we need more than we think we do. We definitely need more than we get.

Chapter Four

Give yourself time and space to heal

Katie is forty-nine. She lives with her partner, eight-year-old son and dog. She is a GP by training, and now runs her own business, a private clinic specialising in women's health.

"*I had my son at forty-one, and at the time I was running a large clinical commissioning unit. There were lots of changes happening within the NHS; it's not always a very nice place to be. On the ground, the clinical teams tend to look out for each other and are very supportive, but within NHS management and the layers of bureaucracy, it's pretty brutal. I'd just come back from maternity leave to a new manager, and three people told me they'd been approached to take over my role while I was off, so I was already feeling quite concerned.*

My passion had always been about joining up healthcare services: bringing together the hospital, the Community Trust and the GP to support patients. Unfortunately, I came back from maternity leave to find a very different ethos. Not long after returning, I was told in a meeting, 'Katie, if you mention "a patient's perspective" one more time, I think you're missing the point of the meeting. We want to know how you manage your budget. We don't care about how things are going to be in five or ten years' time; we care about what's happening now.'

I realised quite quickly that I was becoming detrimental to my organisation because, as a medic in a management role, I was always going to see the bigger picture. Essentially, my new manager wanted someone who could interrogate a balance sheet. I'd take my finance director with me (who could do all these things) to a meeting, but my manager would say: 'I don't want to hear it from your finance director, I want to hear it from you.' It felt wrong; I thought this was a leadership role.

At the time, we were trying to have a second child. My son James had been our second pregnancy. Unfortunately, my first pregnancy had ended at sixteen weeks in a medical termination because the baby had osteogenesis imperfecta, a condition incompatible with life. Understandably, I had been quite anxious during my pregnancy with James, and he hadn't really slept for his first year, so I ended up taking a full year off rather than the six months I had planned. We weren't finding getting pregnant again very easy, and we decided to have investigations, which showed that my ovarian reserve was very low – not surprisingly, as I was forty-two. We decided to try IVF (in vitro fertilisation).

At around the same time, my dad was diagnosed with lymphoma. During tests, he was also found to have bowel cancer. My mum had been suffering increasingly with her mental health, which she managed by drinking, and my dad was the stable one. My dad had his initial treatment, and it looked like it was going to be very successful. He had chemo for the lymphoma and surgery for his gut, and it all looked good. But then his lymphoma returned very aggressively within about three months, and when they did more scans the bowel cancer had spread to his liver. He then became increasingly unwell.

This all happened while I was realising that my job was untenable. I had reached the point where I thought, 'If I don't leave, they're going to get rid of me'. I had a young son, and I wanted to spend time with my dad and be there for him. So I agreed to leave my job. I was sorting out my severance pay and having IVF. My dad was getting sicker very quickly, and because I was a doctor, my family expected that I would know how to manage everything.

Things culminated in a week where I signed my severance agreement, I had a negative pregnancy test after my first round of IVF and my dad died.

All in the same week.

I was devastated by the loss of my dad, but I was trying to see the positives: my narrative was 'Thank goodness I gave up work, because it gave me time with my dad, and I was only trying IVF because I needed to say that I'd explored all the options, so it's not a big deal that it didn't work'. I went back into general practice, working two days a week, considering where to go next with my career. James was at nursery a couple of days a week. I had more time to myself than I'd had in quite a long time.

I felt completely numb. I just plastered on a smile each day. All the things I had to do, I did. I worked extra hard to make sure everything was good for James. I was a good colleague at work, and it was only in the moments I had to myself that I collapsed. I just couldn't deal with it; I couldn't be in my own thoughts at all. I was miserable, but I was good at putting a brave face on it. Even the people around me couldn't see that I was falling apart. We think it's clear when someone is struggling, or about to fall apart, but it's not.

After three or four months, when I was still crying all the way through taking the dog for a walk, I thought I might need a bit of therapy. I remember saying to the therapist, 'Well, you know, the good thing about these three things happening at the same time is that the most important one takes precedence, and you get a free pass for the other two.' She said, 'Do you honestly believe that, Katie?'. It took me a long time and a lot of talking to realise that these three things were equally big things to have happened to me, and unless I spent time working through them all, I wasn't going to come out the other side.

I thought that if I just put my head down and tried harder to keep going, things would be OK. If I got another senior role, if we moved house, if I bought new things, it would make me feel better. But I was just trying to bury what was going on for me in a societal framework that didn't give me the time or space to properly look at these things. And thank God for the professionals who helped me realise how bruised I was from having to leave my job, how I thought that what had happened was all my fault. This was the first time in my life I'd ever really failed. When I look back, I know I didn't fail; I was in an impossible work situation, but I held it all as my issue. I felt I was allowed to grieve for my dad, but I couldn't talk about the work thing because I felt mortified that it had happened to me. I felt equally mortified that I couldn't have a second child because that, too, was my fault. I'd left it too late. And my now son won't have a sibling.

How have we ended up in a place where we have these completely unrealistic, unmanageable expectations of ourselves? If someone else had said the same things to me, I would have thought they were being way too hard on themselves, but I couldn't give myself the same kindness.

Eventually, I felt able to set up my clinic, specialising in women's health, which allowed me to bring together my passion for knitting with the many different aspects of healthcare. It has been fantastic, but it was a hard road getting here. But when I look back, I think that, if it hadn't been for all those things happening at once, I wouldn't have got to know myself as well as I do now."

We all have times when life is hard, and we don't always recognise that this will impact us and what we're able to do. It can be incredibly difficult to recognise that you need help; you might think it's not possible for you, that you have to stay in a state of denial, falling apart quietly inside. But I think we need to realise that you can only hold things together for so long, and then the body says no.

Everyone has a limit, and it can be impossible to spot when you're reaching it until it's too late. Some of us turn to alcohol or drugs, or some other form of self-destruction. Some of us over-exercise as a form of self-punishment. It's too easy to hide from yourself and the people around you. It's not just major trauma that can impact our mental health; it can happen gradually over time – like a chronic, gradual trauma.

And it's normal! Our brains were not designed to make us joyful; they have evolved to keep us safe and alive by looking for danger and bringing it to our attention. This ability to tune ourselves to threats and focus on them above all other thoughts is the reason humans still exist. We evolved over hundreds of thousands of years, living in small communities, only encountering a couple of hundred people in our lifetime. But today we are moving around the big wide world and coming into contact with thousands of people from different backgrounds.[1] We are bombarded with millions of pieces of information every day, and most of it is negative, whether it's a gossip article shaming a celebrity for gaining weight or a news article showing harrowing footage of children being killed. If you think about it, anxiety isn't a disorder at all; it's our brain doing what it was designed for. The problem is our environment.

This was never clearer than during the pandemic. The news started each day with the daily death count. There were headlines about us running out of body bags and pictures of nurses wearing bin bags for protection. It went on for months and months. We were wiping our groceries with antibacterial wipes and not seeing anyone outside our households. We lived in a constant state of fear. The impact on people's mental health was enormous, and I don't think we will ever know the full extent of it.

The problem is, it's not easy to access support. In the UK, 23 per cent of people wait more than twelve weeks for their first appointment following a mental health referral. 43 per cent say the wait makes their mental health worse, and 78 per cent of patients seek help from emergency services.[2]

Being honest with ourselves is the critical first step. It's not shameful to say we're not coping. It's not weak to say we need help, or a rest, or a break from it all. We need to normalise this and make a point of speaking about it openly. We also need to check in on our women, properly, and make sure they're OK. If you are struggling, talk to someone. If you can afford therapy, prioritise it. If you see someone who looks like they're doing really well through a situation that looks unbearable, maybe they're not coping underneath. Maybe they're masking – we do it so well. Reach out to them, not with advice but with your time. Just listen. Sometimes it's the most important thing we can do.

---

1. *New Insights Into Anxiety Disorders:* (Book, 2012) An evolutionary perspective on anxiety and anxiety disorders.
2. Royal College of Psychiatry: (Article, 2022) Hidden waits force more than three quarters of mental health patients to seek help from emergency services.

Chapter Five

Pursue your purpose

Helena is fifty-five. She lives in Hampshire with her husband of thirty years. She has one child and five grandchildren. She is a finance director in the defence industry.

"I'd always assumed I was going to have a large family, not a career. That was who I was going to be: a wife and a mother. I had a baby at sixteen, which was an accidental pregnancy. I had my daughter and did the best I could at that age, continuing to study and get my degree. But I still saw a big family and lots of babies in my future.

When I married my husband aged twenty-six, I stopped using contraception immediately and decided that was it – we're going to have lots of children. I told all my friends that we were trying for a baby. We were excited! But nothing happened.

We did all the normal things. We went to the doctors and had tests, and they confirmed that there was nothing wrong with either of us. It was completely unexplained infertility. Because I'd already had a child, I wasn't entitled to any fertility treatment on the NHS, so we saved up to do it privately.

While we were saving, I started training to be an accountant and found a job I loved. We went to see a private fertility specialist, who told us we probably had a bit of time since there was nothing wrong with either of us. He advised us to let it go naturally for a bit and give it another couple of years. Because I was doing a job I loved, we put it off.

By this time, I was thirty-four, so I should still have been pretty fertile. We decided to try intrauterine insemination (IUI), which is where they stimulate your body to produce more eggs than it is supposed to, then tell you when they are going to release. You have sex naturally, and you've got more chance of getting pregnant because there are more eggs to fertilise. I didn't tell my boss what was going on; he was male and I didn't want to have that conversation with him – in fact, I didn't tell anyone at work. This was only twenty years ago, but at the time you just couldn't. Now you've got fertility leave and policies that make it easier, but you just wouldn't have had the conversation back then, despite the fact that I was injecting hormones every day and having atrocious mood swings.

We did two rounds of IUI and nothing happened, so we decided to try our first round of IVF. As part of this, I had a couple of scans – they scan you all the time to check what your ovaries are doing. One day, in what I thought was a routine consultation, they told me I didn't have enough eggs. That's it. We were done. I was never going to have another child.

I couldn't believe it. This wasn't my life plan. And all I could think was, if I hadn't got that job, if we hadn't waited, if we'd done it two years earlier ... would we be in this situation? Would I have had the child I desperately wanted?

And then, almost immediately after I got this news, my daughter fell pregnant. I was devastated. If it had been a year later, I would have felt differently, but I had not grieved for my loss. While it was true that I had a child, I had been very young when I had her. I hadn't had the experience of being pregnant with a partner who wanted our baby as much as I did. All the things you take for granted – I never did any of them. I was sixteen. I didn't have a clue what I was doing or what was going on. I was the eldest of four, there had been lots of babies in my family, and I knew what to do logistically. I'd decided that I was able to have a child and look after her, but I don't think I was ever a proper, really good mother. I think I did the best I could and that, to some extent, I wanted to have another go just to prove that I could do it.

So my husband has no genetic children. We had a conversation about it. I said, 'You can leave me and find someone you can have genetic children with.' He just said, 'It's unexplained. It could be me. I could go off and find someone else and still not be able to have kids with them, so no!' And now I know he feels very much that he has had the experience of having babies, because my daughter went on to have four more babies. There have been a lot of kids in our lives.

The consequence of my dream being unfulfilled was that my career became everything, because that was what I had instead of a baby. I threw myself into work and I always put it first. I couldn't go to things at the weekend because I had to work, and I was lucky that my husband was happy to do the same. It works for us, but I definitely put work before my child and my grandchildren. And then, a year ago, it all went to hell when I realised my boss no longer thought I was able to do my job. It's always awful to lose your job but, when I felt like I had given up everything for my career, it felt worse. It destroyed my confidence. Even though I took control of my exit, my confidence was on the floor after four or five months of my boss telling me I wasn't good enough. It destroyed me in a way it shouldn't have. I just felt, if I am no good at this, then what am I good at? I don't have anything. But soon enough I got a new job and started to rebuild my confidence.

I look back and wish things were different. They tell you that the average woman is still fertile until their late thirties, that your average cycle is twenty-eight days, your average woman is this or that. But none of us are 'the average woman'.

We are all individuals with our own fertility and cycle. No matter how expert the advice, we must follow our own path and our own instincts.

I wish I hadn't waited."

Purpose is a powerful force that drives us to do amazing things, even against huge odds. When we live with purpose, it gives us clarity and guides our life decisions. It's also a deeply individual and personal thing.

The problem is, we are bombarded with messages about what our lives *should* look like by the media, our families, and even our own constraining thoughts. Many people make bad decisions that stay with them for the rest of their lives. They choose a career that doesn't fulfil them, or a partner who doesn't share their values. Sometimes they don't even realise they've done it until it's too late, and they realise the thing they thought they wanted makes them unhappy.

A hundred things might hold us back from pursuing what we want. Sometimes it's life logistics, and other times it's something deeper, such as a lack of confidence. Helena simply thought she had more time than she had, and her dream went unfulfilled.

Find the thing that excites you and do that. Don't wait. Do not submit to the pressure of those around you. You will never be your best self if you are not happy in what you are doing.

I know this is easy to say, and much harder to do. Sometimes there are very good reasons why we can't do the thing we feel is our purpose. I can't now suddenly decide to become a doctor or a lawyer, nor can I give up my income and family's stability to become an artist or travel the world. But we must find the time and insight to work out what we need, what our soul needs, and make changes that bring us closer to what fulfils us.

Chapter Six

Connect deeply with yourself

Alicia is thirty-nine and lives in Hampshire with her husband and two children age six and four. She works in communications at a public service media broadcast organisation.

" *I could never put my finger on it, but I never felt like I fit in. I looked around at my peers at school, and through university, and always felt like I was faking it to try to be the same as them. Not just in terms of achievements, but also socially. It felt like other people were able to do things in a straightforward way, such as hold down a relationship or a job, and it just felt so difficult for me. But I didn't know why. I had been to my GP so many times through my late twenties and early thirties, and I was brushed off repeatedly. How I felt had always been put down to anxiety or depression, and I tried many things to help: therapy, meds, changing my diet – all the things they tell you to do, but it never felt like anything worked. I felt like I was chasing something.*

In the end, it was social media that helped me see what the issue was. Social media has two sides. It's got these dark corners, and there's a lot of disinformation, which is problematic, but if you're responsible for cultivating your own consumption, it can be a powerful tool for connecting you with other people. Interestingly, I found that having kids gave me permission to explore more about myself – I wanted to be happier and more at peace, because I wanted to be a better mum.

Over time, through reading and hearing stories from other women, I suspected that I might have ADHD (attention deficit hyperactivity disorder). The problem with ADHD is that we have a preconceived idea of manic little boys who can't sit still – that's what I thought ADHD was all about. But I read three or four stories by women my age, and I learned that ADHD presents so differently in women. When I started exploring, it was as if a penny dropped. It was an epiphany moment.

I learned that, for women, ADHD is rarely seen as hyperactivity because little girls, especially those who grew up in the 1980s and 1990s, were conditioned to sit properly, behave nicely, not be bossy. It was OK for little boys to run around and be a bit of a nutter, but not little girls. To survive, girls have to find a way of masking, and they're good at it. The problem is, if you push it down, it doesn't go away – it just finds somewhere else to come out. For women, it tends to manifest in the way we think and feel. The hyperactivity was all in my head. In my head, it was chaos. It always used to make me laugh when people said things like 'I've lost my train of thought'. I used to think, 'I've never had a train of thought! I've literally got 700 trains going in different directions, and if I'm lucky I'll be able to hang on to a thread and say what I want to say.'

At first, I didn't want to talk to anyone. I thought people would judge me, because I had read a few stories on Instagram and now I was jumping on the ADHD bandwagon! I wanted to explore it, and I wanted to get a diagnosis. I went back to my GP armed with all the information I had gathered, and as soon as I mentioned ADHD, it was like I had said a magical password. All those years, doctors had just focused on my anxiety – we had talked about postnatal depression, my hormones, but not once in fifteen years had anyone mentioned neurodiversity. They referred me for an initial assessment but it became clear that the NHS route was going to be very slow. It was 2020 then, and they told me about the next appointment for an ADHD assessment was 2023! Imagine struggling all your life and being told there could be a reason for it, and a treatment, but it couldn't be looked into for three years. It's like some sort of purgatory, just waiting, not knowing what to do or where to go. I went down the private route, which was expensive, and something most people wouldn't be able to do. It's sad that you need money to do that. You get this initial view from the GP, but they just don't know. They haven't been trained in ADHD; they haven't got the money to fund tests and investigations – there's just no one there.

The assessment was intense and took hours and hours. It was done during Covid, so it was all online. Hilariously, during one of the ninety-minute assessments my laptop died and I had to run around to find a charger. Then I realised I'd left the oven on, and I had to take in a delivery that I'd booked to arrive at the same time as my appointment. The psychiatrist must have thought 'This is the easiest diagnosis in the world'!

When I finally got the diagnosis, aged thirty-five, it changed my life. I found a medication that was effective for me, and it's made my life so much better. I did go through a process of grieving. Getting a new piece of information like this about yourself makes you look at things through a different lens, and it changes your memories. I felt sad for six- or seven-year-old me, and wondered if my life would have been different if I'd known. I reflected on my twenties when I'd go for epic twenty-mile runs and tell myself it was because I was into fitness. But it wasn't normal; it was a coping mechanism to calm my brain. I didn't have the education and awareness to know what was actually going on. I reflected on everything – maybe my grades at university would have been better if I'd known. Maybe my first marriage wouldn't have failed.

Feeling like I was different had affected my confidence all my life. I would be so anxious if I knew I was going to be put on the spot, or if I had to talk in front of people, because I found it so hard to articulate things. It's something I've had to do a lot in my professional life – I've been asked my opinion in a meeting or had to introduce myself. It always terrified me! It didn't help that I once got feedback that a presentation I had given had been a "car crash". That's why there's a lot of crossover between ADHD and anxiety. For me, the anxiety was not the cause of my problems; it was the effect of my ADHD. I had always chalked it up to being bad at presenting and would avoid situations, and even not apply for jobs if I thought I would have to do it.

But eventually I came through the grief, and for the first time I had this amazing feeling of forgiving myself. People don't have ADHD because of trauma, or conditioning, or because something in their life triggers it; we are born with our brain like this.

I'm not lazy. I'm not stupid. I'm not clumsy or ditsy or all those things that other people said I was. I conformed to these things because it's easier to lean into it and say 'Yes, I'm the liability, the awkward one'. So, I did. But now I feel calm, knowing all that stuff was nothing I could have controlled. I was working with a completely different set of tools. Of course I was finding it more difficult.

After my diagnosis, I started learning all the amazing things about ADHD. It means your problem-solving skills are incredible! While neurotypical people might go from A to B, I'll zigzag my way there and uncover all these things that would be invisible to others.

Only then did I start to talk about it, and that was an interesting experience. When you tell someone something like that, they want to make you feel better, and it taught me how not to respond when someone tells you something significant. Now, when someone shares something with me, I remind myself not to assume they're devastated, and not to project my own knowledge onto the situation, but just to listen. It's not helpful when you tell someone something and they repeat all the soundbites back at you from their knowledge bank, which is usually limited on something they haven't experienced. Now, I only share my ADHD with people when I know their reaction is going to be something I can handle. I have also found a brilliant community of women dealing with the same issues, either themselves or with their children, and we are learning about it all together."

Like Nia, Alicia found herself navigating a system that didn't serve her. Until as recently as 2020, there was very little research into women with ADHD and how it affects us. Three times as many men were being diagnosed with the condition. Funding, education and resources were (and still are) biased. Only in the past five years has this started to change – but there is still a long way to go to achieve gender parity, leaving millions of women stuck, without information or support, and often suffering in silence.

Women like Alicia are faced with navigating this biased system alone. Treatment options are inaccessible and often ineffective. NHS support is limited and inconsistent. Private treatment is expensive and simply not an option for many.

The lack of understanding of her own self meant that Alicia adopted the limiting labels people gave her – ditsy, clumsy, a liability. When people label us, we start to believe them, and we weave those labels into the fabric of our own identity. It happens to all of us, and it starts as soon as we enter the world and gets worse as we go through school, college, university, work.

But women are becoming wiser to it. We are finding strength and motivation in the systemic flaws that hold us back, and we are pushing for change. Alicia, and many other women, are saying 'Enough!' – and listening to that nagging voice in their head. It's not just about fixing our own problems; it's about finding, or creating, safe spaces where we can be vulnerable and find out who we really are.

Chapter Seven

Childbirth is not "routine"

Amy is a thirty-six-year-old nurse from Cheshire. She lives with her husband and two young children.

"*I was thirty when I had my first baby. I was ready to be a mother. We had tried for a year, and I had an anxious pregnancy because I was nervous every day about losing the baby. I was paranoid at every slowing of the baby's movements, each tiny bit of spotting and the slightest abdominal cramp. By the time my due date arrived, I was desperate for the baby to be here – to have achieved my goal! Naively, I thought the hard part was over and that, as soon as the baby arrived, everything would be perfect.*

By the time I was nine days overdue, I was going out of my mind! I tried all the old home remedies and endured one of the most unpleasant experiences of my pregnancy, a "sweep".

Eventually, I had a long, traumatic labour. I got more and more tired, and after pushing for two hours I finally gave birth to a healthy baby girl. No complications; just a lot of stitches due to third-degree tears. The next day they sent me home with some adult nappies and paracetamol. I wanted to get home and thought that when I did, with all my home comforts, I'd feel better. But I felt horrendous. I had been in labour for three days, and my body had been through a huge trauma. I hurt everywhere. Even my arms and legs ached. I was dehydrated. Every time I moved, the pain from the stitches was unbearable. I found breastfeeding hard, and by day two of struggling to feed, my nipples were cracked and unbelievably sore; I couldn't even wear a soft nursing bra. It got worse and worse over the next couple of weeks until every feed had me in tears. And then my husband went back to work. We had no family support nearby, and I was alone all day. If he had to travel, I was alone all day and all night. I couldn't even go for a wee without the baby screaming to be picked up. Some days I would go all day without even a cup of tea. I couldn't believe how this tiny baby had caused so much physical pain to my body and such chaos in my mind that I couldn't even find time in a day to shower!

But everyone was so smiley and happy, and excited about my baby's arrival. Friends came over with food and gifts and nodded and smiled sagely at the trials and tribulations of having a newborn. I couldn't believe I was expected to just... carry on! Nothing had prepared me for how hard it was. I felt like a failure, like I was supposed to be loving every second. I felt weak at the thought that other women seemed to manage this – and even did it with more than one child.

My recovery was slow, but it did happen. Eventually I regained my strength and my control over my life, and now I look back and wish I had been much kinder to myself during that time. I wasn't a failure; I was just struggling. I wish I had asked for help.

A few years later, after we had our second (which was a much lovelier birth experience), my husband had a vasectomy. He was sent home with a significant amount of advice on self-care, including not to do anything strenuous for two weeks! He was advised to get plenty of sleep, to eat well, and was asked whether there was someone at home who could make sure he had everything he needed so he could 'take it easy' until he felt better! I couldn't believe it! It seemed so unfair. I had been expected to be up all night to feed my newborn, while full of stitches and bleeding, including from my nipples – and I had been expected to be happy about it and filled with joy and gratitude. Nobody had asked me if I had anyone at home to take care of me. Nobody had acknowledged that my body had just undergone something monumental.

Somehow, we have got into the mindset that childbirth is 'routine' – and medically, it is. Women give birth every day. But I don't. It's not routine to me! It was a twice-in-a-lifetime experience. It's like saying being hit by a car is routine because people get hit by cars every day. They do – and sometimes they come off less injured than a woman who has just given birth!"

Childbirth is the ultimate illustration of the power of women. I will forever be in awe of my body for having the capacity to grow another human being with fingers and toes and organs and hair and a personality, and then feeding it with my milk for months.

But it can also be painful – our bodies literally tear apart. We bleed for weeks. We can't go to the toilet without extreme pain. We get sent home with stitches. And we are supposed to just suck it up and be grateful that we have our baby. We no longer have respite centres where women can recover, with specially trained nurses to help them. Instead, we have things like 'baby spin classes' – bring your baby, in their car seat, to spin classes so you can get 'back in shape' quickly.

In many cultures, it is still commonplace for women to have a forty-day period of recuperation after childbirth, when they are supported by friends, family and members of the community. They are given traditional healing foods and supported each day, to allow them to focus on breastfeeding and taking care of themselves. In Latin America, they call it *cuarentena*.

I love this idea. I think it's time we took better care of women after birth, and adjusted our expectations of ourselves to take as long as we need to feel human again. The next time a woman in your life has a baby, go round with food, make her tea, fold the laundry, empty the dishwasher, and hold the baby for an afternoon so she can shower or have a nap. And if you're the one with the baby, ask people to do the same for you. It doesn't mean you're weak or that you aren't coping.

We must stop treating this monumental event in our lives as routine and resist the temptation to rush back to life. Even when we wanted the baby desperately and tried for a long time to become a mother, it's OK to find it hard.

We can be grateful and scared at the same time. We can love our babies more than anything in the world and still find parenting impossible some days. Both things can be true at the same time and it doesn't mean we're not doing it right!

Chapter Eight
Sharing your pain can help others

Chantelle is a forty-nine-year-old project manager. She lives in Dorset with her husband. She has three children: two have flown the nest and one is in secondary education.

"Working for a company that is male dominated has its challenges but, when you enter a new phase in your life, some of the challenges become harder. I realised I was going through perimenopause around two years ago, and I found myself sighing with relief that there was a reason for the way I was feeling.

Looking back, my journey through this phase started in my early forties. I suffered from anxiety, mood swings, brain *fog, insomnia, palpitations and sudden changes in my body temperature, to name a few. I found myself sitting in the toilets at work, crying, feeling like I was no use to anyone. I was thinking of leaving, as I saw myself as a failure: I had lost my ability to communicate effectively in meetings, or to focus... and I was irritated at the smallest of things. I was also having issues at home. Maintaining my composure at work meant more that I released my pent-up emotions at home. I separated myself, hiding away, not wanting to participate in normal activities. I got no enjoyment from anything and felt depression setting in. There was no escape from my situation and no safe place.*

When I was finally helped by my doctor to understand what was happening, it was like a light had been turned on, but even finding out wasn't an easy task. I had to find a doctor who was open-minded and who wasn't just going to prescribe antidepressants. Knowing that I was in perimenopause, I could start looking for ways to help myself.

I started my journey to find combinations of self-help and medication that worked for me, to help me find my new me. I changed my exercise regime and looked at my mental wellbeing. But the game-changer was being able to explain to my friends and family that I was on a journey, and that what I had been going through was for a reason; that I had not changed into a horrid person who was unrecognisable to them – and myself.

One day at work, I was talking about my experience with female colleagues, making a joke of some of the things I was going through. I was highlighting the importance of acknowledging symptoms and not just accepting that you have no options. I was sharing my experience and answering questions as best I could. At this moment, I realised I could offer so much more: I could help prevent other women feeling the loneliness and isolation I had felt many months before. A colleague I didn't know well asked if she could join in our conversation. She too was feeling lost on this journey, not knowing where to start, how to wade through all the information.

I had a strong feeling that I wanted to help. I decided I would approach the site manager to see if he would support me to create an informal coffee club to bring women together to support each other and learn more about this taboo topic.

He was really encouraging. I was over the moon that the business was open to supporting its female staff in this way. I organised an informal coffee morning, encouraging people to come and talk about all things menopause. And twenty-two people came to our first session – men and women of all ages. They wanted to know how they could support their colleagues, family members and partners. Some asked me about my journey, some shared their own. We shared remedies, but remained open-minded to the fact that one size does not fit all. It was exciting but also scary. I was outside my comfort zone but, with the support of colleagues, we have now held several sessions. I reached out further within the business and have supported other colleagues to hold their own coffee mornings in their workplaces.

It's not easy. Some women don't want to talk about it, and we must respect this. Some people make mean comments that we are using the menopause as an excuse for being inadequate or lazy. We can't stop this; all we can do is raise awareness of the menopause and all the symptoms women might experience. It is a time of life when we must look for ways to work with the changes our bodies are going through, accept we cannot return to what was and recognise that we are a new kind of beautiful. In Japan, they refer to the menopause as 'the second spring', so let's embrace this in the UK too. We need to be kind, listen, support each other and be patient, as all women will need something different to help us through this time."

Menopause is often poorly understood, even by women, because we put it in a category that doesn't apply to us – at least, not yet. It's scary and taboo, because it signals the end of our fertility – the thing that makes us youthful and desirable. It's wider waistlines, flat shoes and portable fans. Happily, there is a lot more awareness about the menopause these days, thanks to people such as Davina McCall and medical experts such as Dr Louise Newson. However, it is still not widely discussed among young women in the same way that puberty is. We are expected to work it out for ourselves. But it changes everything about our bodies, our minds, and our lives.

I was lucky enough to spend some time with Dr Katie, a doctor who specialises in women's health, who shared this awesome advice:

"Pick your sources of information carefully. It's easy to think that Instagram or Facebook are your primary sources of information, but the truth is that anyone can set up camp there and put their opinions forward as expert advice. I would steer clear of these and instead go to trusted sources. The patient arm of the British Menopause Society is called Women's Health Concern. They have very well-written patient fact sheets and videos. Another is a website called Rock My Menopause, which is the patient arm of the Women's Health Foundation. It provides well-balanced information.

Don't follow a million menopausal women on Instagram! You'll end up getting confused and seeing such polarised opinions. You are more than your menopause. You don't want to spend every waking moment reading about it. Remember that you don't have to know everything. You don't have to be your own doctor – you just need the basic information on how your body works.

Do your research before going to see your GP. Find out whether someone in your GP practice has an interest in the menopause. This might be a nurse rather than a doctor. Ask to see them. Before your appointment, write all your thoughts down so you can think clearly without being under time pressure. List all your symptoms and why you think they are menopause-related and set out all your questions. Your doctor can't read your mind – write down all the things you are worried about, so you're not put on the spot in the appointment.

If you're going to take HRT, try not to think that there is a 'right' and a 'wrong' one. It's about finding a medicine that works for you and that fits with your lifestyle. There's no use being given a gel if you don't have time to make using it part of your routine. If the only time you can apply it is right before you get dressed, so it mostly goes into your clothes, that's not going to work for you. You're allowed to ask for a second opinion if you're not satisfied with the outcome.

Have a follow-up review after three months. If this isn't offered, book it with your doctor. Use the time to discuss how the medicine is working for you, any side effects, and make sure you are using it properly. Also book an annual review – and don't let it become a tick-box exercise to check your blood pressure. Talk about anything that's concerning you and ask any questions you have.

If you can access private healthcare, consider going to a specialist clinic. You will see someone quickly and have time with them beyond a ten-minute appointment. You will access all the same things via the NHS, but you might need to wait a bit longer, and you won't have the luxury of time with a specialist. The private route gives you time to have a nuanced conversation, which can be incredibly helpful. For the cost of a haircut, the appointment might change your life!"

Part 2 – Work

Chapter Nine

Times have changed... kind of

Priya is a forty-two-year-old mum of three. She works as a corporate lawyer for a food and drink manufacturer. She lives with her husband and kids in Birmingham.

"We were in my kitchen waiting for the royal wedding to start – the William and Kate one. Not being royalists, we just wanted to watch it for the pomp and spectacle, and to see Kate's dress! We live in a multigenerational household with my husband's parents, and my mother-in-law and I had it on in the kitchen while we made tea and chatted.

When Kate stepped out of the car and turned to walk up the stairs to Westminster Abbey, my mother-in-law (a very traditional woman of Indian heritage) gasped, clapped her hands and said to my five-year-old daughter: 'Oh, just imagine, Maddie! One day, you could be a bride! You could walk down the aisle in a beautiful dress and marry the man of your dreams. Wouldn't that be amazing?'

Without wanting to sound too unkind, but knowing I had to intervene, I said something along the lines of 'Yes, or you could be prime minister or run your own business. That would be cool too, wouldn't it?'

I think my mother-in-law thinks I'm some sort of raging feminist, but I just couldn't let it lie. It's been a source of tension between us since I had our first baby. She has suggested, on more than one occasion, that I shouldn't have gone back to work. She has asked me why I work when my husband earns enough to enable me not to. The kids would obviously be better off at home with me, rather than being in childcare.

It was difficult to have these discussions with both her and my own mother, especially in the early days post-childbirth when I was tired and vulnerable. Even now, it's hard not to feel like, no matter how successful I am professionally, the grandparents of my children would have been prouder of me if I was at home in an apron – that my professional success is somehow a failure. Whenever I say I'm tired or under pressure, all I get is thin-lipped judgement and advice to 'just get myself a little job'.

This is the discontinuity. It's not her fault that the pinnacle of achievement for her generation was getting married, and there's nothing wrong with that, if that's what you want for your life! But my daughter doesn't need to be subject to that conditioning. She doesn't need to watch Disney movies about beautiful thin girls who have crappy lives until a man saves them by kissing them without asking for their consent. I want her to be inspired to pursue intellectual and spiritual fulfilment. If that means getting married and raising a family, that's great. But it doesn't have to mean that."

The rising number of women in the workforce has been one of the most remarkable societal and economic changes of the past century. However, female participation is still lower than male participation in every single country in the world. In countries with low female participation (such as Iran, Saudi Arabia and Algeria), numbers tend to be much higher among young women, suggesting a generational shift.[1]

History is not our friend here. All around the world, countries have placed restrictions on women and their ability to work, and it continues to this day. Globally, over 2.7 billion women are legally prevented from doing the same work as men, and 69 countries still have laws limiting women's access to work. In Argentina, a woman can't distill or sell alcohol. Russia has a staggering 455 restrictions on women doing certain jobs, including driving trains. As recently as 2013, Vietnam banned women from driving tractors with engines over 50 horsepower.

Unsurprisingly, women are less likely to work, particularly in leadership positions, where there is no legislation protecting them from sexual harassment. Forty-three countries have no such legislation[2] and, incredibly, 123 countries have no laws to protect women and girls from sexual harassment in an education setting.[3]

Across the English-speaking world, for many decades there were laws to prevent women from working after they were married. These so-called marriage bars were common from the late nineteenth century all the way up to the 1970s, and they called for women's jobs to be terminated upon their marriage. The logic was that married women were supported by their husbands so they didn't need to work. They were labelled 'pin-money workers', because the money they earned was for them to spend on fancy, frivolous things – and their working took away opportunities for men to earn money for their families. This also served as justification for paying women (especially working-class women) lower wages than men.

Since the 1960s, as anti discrimination laws have become more widespread, marriage bars have been outlawed: the last marriage bar to be removed was in Ireland in 1973. However, in eighteen countries around the world, a husband can still prevent his wife from working if he chooses.

The impact of societal views on women working can still be felt, even here in the relatively safe haven of the UK. While our legislation has shifted to outlaw discriminatory practices, there's no doubt that bias still exists within our own support networks and in the workplace. Women of colour are even more disadvantaged, despite being just as ambitious, as they often deal with intersectional bias. I have felt it myself in the industries I have worked in, and particularly in construction and defence.

Women of working age today are on the leading edge of this cultural change, particularly in less progressive industries. Today (in 2024), only twenty-one CEOs in the FTSE350 are women, and only 35 per cent of senior and middle management positions are filled by women.[4]

We need to change the status quo. If we don't, we will never achieve an equal society. Ensuring that women have the opportunity to gain financial and intellectual independence is, in my mind, one of the biggest gifts we can give to the next generation of women and girls.

---

1. Our World in Data: (Article, 2024) Women's employment.

2. World Bank Group: (Report, 2023) Women, business and the law.

3. World Bank Group: (Article, 2018) More than 1 billion women lack legal protection against domestic sexual violence.

4. FTSE Women Leaders: (Report, 2024) FTSE women leaders review.

Chapter Ten

Reach for your inner confidence

Hayley is a medical doctor. She grew up internationally but has lived in the UK since her university days. She has worked as a hospital doctor for over ten years and has recently completed a PhD. She is now a diabetes consultant and a proud mum of two young boys.

"*I*'d always wanted to do medicine; it had been a very clear path for me from GCSE stage. I moved to London for medical school, and it was extremely competitive. There were about 500 people in my year. I was part of a large majority of women, which is contrary to all previous generations of medics. I never felt disadvantaged in any way *being female, but I was aware of the very aggressive and competitive nature of the medical school. People would rip pages out of textbooks before exams to prevent other students from learning aspects of the curriculum. People would be in tears before exams. If you were studying with someone and shared information with someone else, it was as if you had let them down, because you were sharing knowledge that was secret. It was a very bizarre experience.*

I was ranked highly at medical school so I had a choice about where I wanted to work. I didn't like the elitism of London and was keen to leave once I qualified. I didn't want to practise in that environment. A lot of the consultants had nervous tics and were clearly under a lot of pressure. I was lucky that I knew early on that I wanted to specialise in diabetes and endocrinology, which is what I do now.

For my first few years as a junior doctor, I worked in a hospital on the south coast. I enjoyed it there; it was very different. People wanted to share knowledge. I ended up doing all my postgraduate exams quickly because people were very supportive of me. I took any opportunity offered to me and made a lot of good friends, who are my closest friends now. I found that lots of book knowledge is not enough. It can never replace what you learn clinically when you're doing the job.

Around this time, I did my first big practical exam. It would give me credentials as a competent hospital doctor and allow me to go on to specialty training. It's extremely competitive and very subjective. It was the hardest thing I've ever done. I've never worked so hard! But passing that allowed me to specialise and move into a five-year programme, which would move me around hospitals over five years. I was confident in what I'd learned, and keen to move into the specialty I had my heart set on.

Suddenly, I was a specialist in a small hospital in Hampshire. I was being given referrals and thinking, 'What the hell?! I know a lot about this subject but what do I actually do?!' Unfortunately, I worked for two male consultants who found every opportunity to belittle me. They could see I was very keen, but they challenged me in a very aggressive way and gave me no support at all. In my second week, when I was still finding out where everything was in the hospital and trying to remember my logins for the different systems, I was asked to stand in for one of the consultants who wasn't able to take his clinic. It was a maternal diabetes and endocrine clinic (women in pregnancy with diabetes and hormonal problems), which was something I had never done before. It was set to start at 9 a.m., and they told me at 8.30 a.m.

I initially went to the wrong part of the hospital, so by the time I found the right place I was late, and already on the back foot. I had to use a different system for taking notes, because it was part of the maternity system, which I had no idea about. The clinic was with a midwife, and I'd been given no guidance about how to conduct the consultation, such as who takes the lead and who makes the decisions. All the labs were different, and I had no idea what to do. It was horrendous. But I had to be there for the patients – they needed me to be there for them. There are many times in medicine when you might not be 100 per cent confident, but you need to be confident for the person in front of you, especially if you have to have a difficult conversation or discuss a sensitive issue.

Afterwards, I spoke to my consultant. I learned very quickly that I had been thrown in like that to make me feel like a fool and it just got worse from there. They didn't give me the right tools to do my dictations. While they had offices and dictaphones to dictate their notes quickly at the end of each patient, I was given a little school desk with no dictaphone or computer – nothing at all. I would stay late every day trying to finish all my dictations because I knew I wouldn't remember everything once the notes were taken away at the end of the day. When I raised this to one of the consultants, they told me to speak to human resources (HR), who told me I needed to learn better time management!

You have to do a lot of reflection in your training portfolios, to talk about your experiences, and to make sure you're making progress, but I never felt in a safe enough space to do this. In my assessments and feedback, I was regularly told that I lacked confidence, and I even considered taking courses to build my confidence, but I knew that wasn't the issue. I knew that in the right environment I could be confident – outside work, with my family and friends, or if I was advocating for a patient. But when I presented myself to these consultants, they made me feel like a little girl, like a child. They talked down to me and used a lot of belittling humour. They made jokes that I couldn't even respond to, they were so inappropriate. They made me feel small. It was one of the most challenging years of my life.

I regularly went home to my now-husband in tears. The consultants made me feel like I didn't know anything. I internalised all of it. They destroyed my confidence, and I was filled with self-doubt. I even got to the point that I didn't know if I wanted to continue specialty training any more.

Luckily, my terrible experience was followed by a really rewarding year. I moved to a different hospital and had a consultant who, after a while, I trusted enough to confide in about my experience. She helped me see that it wasn't my confidence that was the issue. She even encouraged me to do my specialty exams early, because she could see I had the knowledge. I asked her questions and she would enjoy helping me research particular areas. She was very particular, which I liked: I knew where I stood with her. I learned how she liked to work and made sure I did those things. She encouraged me, and I did well in my specialty exams – partly thanks to her support. Even though she didn't have any more time than the previous consultants, she made the time. She wanted to support me. When someone takes the time to invest in you, it goes such a long way and it can even change how you see yourself."

In my own career, as a senior woman in a male-dominated industry, even today I hear stories about terrible behaviour – from the petty and irritating to the downright illegal.

I myself continue to experience situations where I am treated differently because I am a woman. Very recently, I had a customer who would not have a one-to-one meeting with me to avoid 'accusations of impropriety'. I have had inappropriate sexual comments made to me by senior people in positions of power. I have been talked down to, belittled and patronised. It's particularly hard when it's subtle and could easily be brushed off as a misunderstanding. Nobody wants to be labelled 'an over-sensitive woman' or to be known as 'trouble'.

Many women in the medical profession describe being treated differently to their male colleagues; being asked to bring blankets or refreshments to a patient more often than male colleagues are asked to. They also talk of dealing with assumptions by patients that they are nurses or non-medical members of the team, and of having to assure patients that, yes, they are the doctor. They report both verbal and physical harassment – not just from their colleagues but from patients too. Female patients can have a chaperone if they are alone with a doctor, but female doctors don't get the same protection.

These moments, even the tiny ones, can impact our confidence and self-worth. The actions taken by other people – because of their weaknesses and failures – can be internalised and turned into weaknesses and failures of our own.

But how do you deal with this when challenging the behaviour can have a detrimental impact on your relationships and even your career? It can feel futile – you're never going to change the army, your company, the NHS, society. But not challenging these comments can play havoc with your moral compass. I know that when I have let something slide in the past, I have been left feeling powerless and angry. What do we do? Do we just accept it? How can I teach my kids to speak up when they see injustice, while I let it slide? I'm afraid I don't have the answers, but I have found peace in trying to do a few things.

I set the tone. Whenever someone uses the generic male ('We will recruit a project manager, and *he* will...'), I correct them. This annoys some of my team, who do it without thinking and certainly without any malicious intent. But I correct them every single time. Sometimes I do it in a jokey way. But it's something people now know about me – that I take this stuff seriously – and I think this changes the way people deal with me. I put feminist books on my desk at work and share them with my female colleagues. I make a point of shutting down any sexual 'banter' in my team. They might think I'm boring. I don't really care. My priority is making sure I create a safe working environment where everyone feels supported.

I find allies – and I make sure I am one. When something happens, and I don't feel able to challenge it, I seek support from others. Sometimes just talking things over helps me work out what I should do about it. A couple of times, I've decided I need to say something and have followed up after the fact. It's hard to do but – handled in the right way – it can be even more effective, because you are acting calmly and have time to prepare what you want to say. I make sure that all the women around me know that I am there for them if they need me, and I treat these relationships and conversations with the utmost care and respect. Being a safe space for women to come to when they need it is one of the most rewarding things I get to do at work.

Chapter Eleven

Know your own strength

Katherine is twenty-nine and lives in Gloucestershire. She is an engineer and works in an all-male team in a large British engineering business.

"'You need to toughen up.' I've been on the receiving end of this sentence numerous times in my career so far, mostly due to my inability to stand by and watch unacceptable behaviour.

While it used to make me question my ability and suitability to a life in engineering, as I've got older, I've realised that the person saying these words knows nothing about me. To most people I am sensitive, happy, jovial, probably a little bit silly. And it's true: I am all those things. However, I also struggle with self-doubt, low self-esteem, and all the other issues that come with having low confidence. Balancing the need to please people with my emotional sensitivity and drive to succeed can be difficult. Being someone whose response to frustration is to cry can also be difficult – but I am now learning to accept that, just because my emotions run close to the surface, it doesn't mean I'm not tough.

At fourteen, I was hospitalised for ten months and told I had two months to live if something didn't change. My mum's cancer diagnosis two years before had triggered a huge anxiety in me, associated with the uncertainty of the situation and losing Mum. I cared for Mum through her treatment while trying to maintain a strong academic record and support my family by running the house. As a coping mechanism, I became anorexic – and that is what led me to hospital.

There is no overnight fix for mental ill-health. I was lucky to have a supportive family who stood by me, even when I had given up all hope. It would be ten more years, during which time I lost four friends to anorexia, before I reached a healthy weight. Now, I don't focus on the illness being a sign of weakness but see it as a sign of my resolve and resilience to keep going and never give up.

My mum recovered from the cancer, which I'm forever grateful for; many families are not so lucky. But it wasn't long before *she hit a second hurdle in the form of mental ill-health, resulting in her hospitalisation for seven months. Again, I picked up the role of 'mum' in the home, juggling education with looking after the home – and my own difficulties. This was perhaps the darkest period of my life.*

When I was eighteen, Mum told me she didn't love me and that she couldn't believe she had given birth to me. But through her multiple suicide attempts, it was me she wanted around her. Again, thankfully, she survived. Although we never fully regained the mum we knew and loved, we learned to love this new version of her, and to be grateful that she was still with us.

We both still struggle. I battle destructive thoughts daily, but I have learned that life is a fantastic gift. I've been incredibly lucky to spend time with family and friends, to travel, to experience things I never thought would be possible.

I often wonder how on earth I got to where I am today: a female engineer working with a supportive team, with health, happiness... and a mortgage! The truth is, a handful of people believed in me and never gave up – and, ultimately, I never gave up on myself. I am grateful to my family for loving me unconditionally, and to my university lecturers for taking a chance on me, having left school with a less-than-ideal set of qualifications. I'm grateful to colleagues who see the potential in me and are supportive. Lastly, and I find this extremely hard to say, but I am grateful to myself for having the resilience to keep fighting on and unlocking all the wonderful things life has to offer. It sounds clichéd, but things do get better.

Holding on to my emotions and humanity is something I celebrate, as I believe that kindness and humility have their place in business, no matter how 'tough' the environment is.

So, every time I hear 'you need to toughen up', I smile to myself and reflect on how hard I have fought to be where I am now; their perception of 'tough' says more about them than it does about me. Like I said before, if they think I need to toughen up, they clearly don't know me at all."

Women in all environments are compared to a set of expectations that were developed for yesterday's world. Katherine is a wonderful, energetic, incredibly bright young woman. The people around her are making assumptions about her without realising she has fought some dark and difficult enemies that would probably have broken most people.

Everyone has a blueprint in their mind of what "strong" looks like, what "a leader" looks like, what "a mother" looks like. These blueprints hold us back. If a woman is emotional about something she is passionate about, does that make her less able to withstand the pressure of her job? If she is hard-nosed and mean to people, does that make her strong? I was once advised by an previous boss not to bake a cake for my team meeting, as it might make my colleagues see me as "too mumsy"!

These biases and blueprints get in the way of us bringing all the best things about being a woman to work. They make us bend ourselves out of shape to fit in or conform.

We need to talk more openly about the brilliant, beautiful natural traits women bring to our workplaces and homes. Women tend to be excellent collaborators, good communicators and nurturing of the collective.[1] We can create environments where people feel valued, empowered and more likely to share their ideas. We are more likely to seek out diverse opinions and perspectives, and tend to be more open to feedback, both of which are likely to lead to better outcomes.[2] In all environments, but particularly in high-performance environments where teams are doing hard things under pressure, this can be a buffer that helps the team achieve great things – without compromising mental health or job satisfaction.

Using our natural traits, we can create wonderful working environments where people want to do their very best work, and support people through difficult times. We just have to stop expecting women to behave like men, or be something that makes them less.

---

1. *Harvard Business Review*: (Article, 2018) In collaborative work cultures, women carry more of the weight.
2. McKinsey & Company: (Report, 2020) Diversity wins.

Chapter Twelve

It's not you, it's them

Lola is forty-five and lives in the Midlands with her husband Kyle. She has worked in a range of public service roles and now works in a government contracting organisation.

"*I joined the fire service when I was twenty-one and have worked in traditionally male-dominated environments my whole career. While I have predominantly found the experience of being female in male environments empowering and conducive to discovering my authenticity, there is a particular experience that regularly comes to mind that felt the opposite.*

When I was twenty-three, I was promoted into a youth engagement manager role, where I was responsible for setting up and delivering a Prince's Trust scheme for a major UK emergency service. It was a high-profile project, the first of its kind, and required significant senior engagement at the service headquarters. This was new to me. Up to this point, I had always been part of a wider team. At the beginning of the project, a male colleague and I were appointed to deliver the project together.

My colleague was an experienced operational firefighter who had a lot of experience with community engagement. In our early meetings with senior stakeholders, it quickly became apparent that they did not value his headstrong style. Meetings were often combative and uncomfortable, and I found this experience upsetting and unsettling. Senior officers in the service wear a very formal uniform, and the culture in the organisation at that time was very hierarchical, not used to including a wide range of views.

My colleague was soon removed from the project and not replaced, and I found myself leading the project on my own, without a team and without a sponsor that I felt psychologically safe with. Engaging senior staff was left to me, and even now I find it difficult to explain how intimidating I found it. I didn't have anyone to guide me in understanding the expectations of the group. I found myself in a boardroom full of senior men in official uniforms, often with new people that I had never met and wasn't introduced to. Sometimes, I would find myself crying in the toilet either before or after these meetings, or even during the meeting (I still feel *embarrassed admitting that). I think about that young woman and am angry at an organisation that couldn't recognise the signs of visible distress. They were unable to adapt their approach or recognise the need to provide greater professional support. When I try to put my finger on it, this is what I get to: the group valued the work I was doing (I know this to be true, from the success of the project and recognition further down the line), but I also think they enjoyed the feeling of power they got from knowing that I was intimidated by them. There is something desperately sad about a group of middle-aged senior men feeling powerful about having a solitary, non-operational young female answering to them.*

After about a year, a new female manager was appointed, and my experience with her was perhaps even more disappointing. She encouraged me to 'jump on the coat tails of one of the senior men who was likely to be promoted, to ensure success in my future career'. Her guidance extended to telling me to act in a deferential manner in formal situations, not to speak up and to be very respectful to the men around me. Suffice to say, I quickly learned the type of manager I didn't want to be!

Sadly, I've seen this unsupportive approach from women in other workplaces. Some women who have worked hard to achieve and be recognised in the workplace tread on other women who are trying to walk the same path. They don't use their success to encourage and value inclusivity. I think this comes from a place of insecurity and a sense of inferiority, but to watch women behave as if they are the only one allowed in the club is utterly heartbreaking. Probably the worst thing about it is that it reinforces the culture, particularly in male-dominated environments, that makes breaking through so difficult in the first place. A vicious cycle.

As I have grown older and experienced different ways of working, I recognise the value in being vulnerable at work. I don't worry if colleagues, managers or teams see me visibly upset or ecstatically happy. Work is such a huge part of our lives; I don't believe I could be any other way without seriously impacting my mental health. I have also learned a lot about unhealthy culture and how to avoid this, and I think I have used this learning to my benefit – and to benefit those around me."

Bad behaviour at work can be even more damaging when it comes from other women. I experienced some of this in my time in construction, in the early part of my career. There were very few women in senior roles within that organisation at the time. The ones that had made it had clambered their way up through the mire of misogyny and probably experienced some horrible behaviour along the way. But, against all odds, they had made it. I used to think that they ought to feel some sort of duty to support other women, but it seemed to be the opposite. Some of them wanted to be the only woman in the boardroom – as if it was a badge of honour, something they had earned. Maybe it made them feel special. In any case, it made them nasty. They were aggressive and intimidating and seemed to particularly enjoy putting other women in their place. We used to call them chicks with dicks. Perhaps all their compassion had been chipped away by the hostile environment they had grown up in. Perhaps they had been forced to squash down their humanity to survive. Who knows?

Several academics have named this behaviour the 'queen bee phenomenon':[1] senior women distancing themselves from junior women and behaving in a stereotypically more masculine way. Unfortunately, women are sometimes encouraged to behave this way, especially in male-dominated environments that value and reward certain behaviours, no matter how damaging these are to the culture and the people within it.

I am lucky to have some incredible female friends, mentors and colleagues. But I also know that, sadly, in all walks of life and at all stages of life, some women love to tear each other down. Stay-at-home mums judge working mums for leaving their kids in childcare. Working mums judge stay-at-home mums for not working. I have been subject to the judgement of other women countless times over the years – sometimes implicit and sometimes explicit! I was once asked on the school playground by another mum why I bothered having kids if I was going to have them raised by a nanny.

Surely the whole point of feminism was to give women the freedom to choose what we want to do with our lives? Now we can choose, but we love to judge each other's choices – just read the comments on any woman's Instagram feed when she shares anything about her life.

Sometimes the factor driving this judgement is fear, insecurity, self-doubt or jealousy. Several years later, I heard the same woman who had berated me for working full-time talking to her friend about how frustrated she was that she wasn't making the most of the master's degree she had worked so hard for. Let's think twice before we judge each other. Instead, let's celebrate the huge journey we have been on as women to get where we are, and recognise that millions of women in the world don't have the privilege of choice, and support each other whether we approve or not.

---

1. *The Leadership Quarterly*: (Journal, 2016) The queen bee phenomenon: Why women leaders distance themselves from junior women.

Chapter Thirteen

Be where you can thrive

Laura is forty-four and lives in West Sussex with her husband and five-year-old son. She is a self-employed management consultant and has been working in transformation and change for twenty-five years.

"*I had a major burnout moment when I was thirty-seven. I was working as the transformation director for a fintech (financial technology) company – not necessarily known for being the most supportive working environment. I was in a role I felt comfortable with, because I knew the space well. While I was in a new environment, it didn't feel outside my skill set or capability.*

What I found was a challenging organisation, and a lot of people in senior roles who didn't understand what the transformation was all about. They wanted something different to what they had employed me to do. My job was very visible at an exec level but had been very poorly thought through. I had to do a lot of influencing early on to reset staff expectations. I got on well with my boss and my peers, and had a huge amount of respect from the people around me, including my team, but I struggled with the senior people. I bumped up against the CEO and CFO, and I didn't get support from my boss. He would agree something with me before a meeting with the CEO, then buckle in the meeting, leaving me to have the difficult conversation with the CEO. Basically, he threw me under the bus. The behaviour became increasingly toxic.

I ended up moving into a different part of the business. It was a lateral move, but I knew the leader and joined his team. In this new environment, I got a confidence boost because the team I had inherited was pleased I was there: they were glad to have someone leading them who understood the environment and what they did. I made a big impact with them in a short time, and I really built the team up. Then out of the blue I got an email from my boss that said some changes were happening and I had to go and work in another department, and hand over all the good work I had done to another manager. It wasn't what I wanted. I wasn't OK with it.

I spoke to my boss, and he said, 'Laura, you know, I could fight it if you want, but that's probably not the best thing. You should probably just go along with it.' So I agreed to it. To this day I still kick myself, because the new role felt very hollow. I didn't own anything, I didn't have a team, I just felt I was on the periphery. There were days when I didn't have anything to do and nobody asked me to do anything. I'd gone from being a central cog in the organisation to being sidelined. In some ways, I was happy not to have to deal with the senior team, but I didn't feel valued. I realised then that I need to feel part of things.

That period coincided with a time when I was trying to get pregnant. We had been trying for three years, and I was getting more and more disheartened and frustrated.

I started getting some odd health issues. I sometimes felt dizzy and lightheaded. I would get uncontrollably weepy, and some days I just didn't want to do anything. I'd always been able to handle stress, yet now, little things were getting to me. And what was surprising was that the stress came during a period when I wasn't in demand. I had no deadlines or big things I had to do. It was like a cumulative stress. The stress of not feeling like I had a place in the organisation. Decisions were being made about things that impacted me, and I was not involved in those decisions. I was desperate to leave, but I couldn't find the motivation to look for another job.

Somehow, I don't think anyone noticed. I still showed up. I'd work from home, look at my computer screen, run the occasional team meeting, and respond to emails. I was very good at masking. I was still operating.

When I reflect on it now, I stayed because I thought, 'I can do this. I am successful and I always make it work.' I was desperate to make it work. I hadn't identified clearly enough the signs of the toxic culture I was in.

The combination of work and things outside work built up until, one day, I felt as if I was at my wits' end. I needed some space. Even though I wasn't in demand at work, I needed to switch off the computer and be at home for a bit. I needed to totally disengage, and I needed to talk to someone who could help me.

I told my boss I needed to be signed off work for two weeks. I didn't even tell him why, just that I had a health issue. I didn't expand on it and he didn't ask! I felt so embarrassed asking for time off. I always felt that going off for stress was a real sign of weakness, a sign of not being able to do your job, but I knew I needed to step back.

I'm very action-orientated: when I realised I was depressed, I went into practical mode and considered what I needed to do next. During my time off, I decided I had to leave. I wasn't going to make it work there, and the personal cost was too high.

I stayed in the organisation for eight months after that. It took me a while to extricate myself. I ended up managing my own exit through a redundancy process. But, again, I didn't tell people I was made redundant, because that felt like a failure too, even though it was a decision I had made. It was a way of wrestling back control.

During this, I got pregnant, so I had something important to look forward to. But that meant I wasn't focused on getting a new job. I was finishing in April and my son was due in August. I was thinking about time off and maternity leave.

On my last day as an employee, even though I hadn't turned my computer on for about three weeks by this point, I felt incredibly anxious. This intense anxiety lasted two or three weeks. Right up until my job ended, I felt like it all made sense: I've got lots to look forward to, I'm going to get paid redundancy, I'm going to have my baby. But then it felt like going over a cliff edge. My job had gone. I had let go of something important – my corporate identity as a professional woman, and it was gone indefinitely, because I didn't have a job to go back to. I didn't know what the other side of this looked like – having a baby and being a mum who didn't work. It was terrifying.

Around a year after having my baby, I started coming back into work, in my own consulting practice. It probably took me a year after that to fully regain my confidence."

Making a positive change in your life is a hard, gutsy thing to do, particularly if you have commitments and obligations to other people, and especially if your sense of self-worth and purpose has been eroded by the situation you are in. It can feel like you're on a carousel and can't get off. Stepping off might not be an option for a million reasons: the mortgage, commitments or simply because our work has become central to our own identity.

Big changes often happen after a crisis or a significant event in your life, something that makes you look at the world differently and forces you to change your life. Sometimes it's more subtle than this: self-reflection during dog walks, long talks with a good friend or just reflecting on what's making us happy or unhappy.

Deciding to change something big in your life is one thing. Enacting it and making it work is something else. Making change successfully is much easier if you have a strong support network: a team of supporters who will help you work through the knotty bits and support you when you wobble.

When we want to change jobs, we're given a ton of advice that may or may not be helpful, like 'It's easier to find a job when you've got a job.' But there's no "right" way to change your career or change your life. There's no set path or manual to follow. You get to create your own rules and carve out your own unique journey.

Don't stay in an organisation that doesn't fit you. Think carefully about finding a job, team or company based on your values and what you need to grow. It's not always obvious in an interview or in the early days when you're in a new environment, but if it's not right you will know it soon enough.

Like Laura, you might find that one of the first clues is feeling like you're doing a bad job, particularly when you're doing things you usually consider yourself to be good at. It can feel like no matter what you do, it's not quite right. Or you might feel like you have to work harder than normal to get the same result. You might get feedback that surprises you, like you need to work on your confidence, your time management, your presentation skills. But maybe it's not you at all – maybe you're that square peg in a round hole. Early in my career, I was told 'You need to smooth down your rough edges.' I remember thinking, 'I quite like my rough edges, actually!'

Shortly after this I moved from financial services to work in construction, where my rough edges were exactly what I needed to thrive!

If you can, pay attention to signs that your organisation is wrong for you, and act.

Chapter Fourteen

The motherhood penalty

Emily is twenty-nine and lives in London with her husband Tom and daughter Harriet. She works in a major marketing agency.

"When I found out I was pregnant, I felt both excitement and trepidation. My husband and I had been married for eighteen months and were delighted. I had just been promoted to account manager at the busy marketing company I had been at for eight years, which was growing, and full of young, trendy graduates. The office, in central London, was everything you might imagine: fake grass and ping-pong tables. Beautiful people in skinny jeans and high heels. I loved it and made a great group of friends there.

Even before I started telling people about my pregnancy, things felt different at work. I couldn't join in the Friday after-work drinks. I had terrible morning sickness, which left me feeling lousy and looking washed out. I waited as long as I could before I started to tell people, but eventually I needed to start going to antenatal appointments – and, to be honest, I couldn't hide my bump any longer. At twelve weeks, I told my manager and the team I worked with. Almost immediately, their attitudes towards me shifted. Some of the younger team members even reacted to my news with something like sympathy – not quite 'Oh, I'm sorry to hear that', but almost. Some were supportive. Others treated me differently, whether intentionally or not. A lot of people felt the need to offer unsolicited advice about childbirth, parenting and even what to eat.

Worse than this, I was gradually sidelined from key projects. I had been a top performer for the eight years I had been there and was regularly given the toughest projects to work on. Despite showcasing my capability throughout my tenure, I quickly became seen as fragile, or less capable. I felt as if people were underestimating my professional competence. It wasn't malicious but I felt it every day. Despite my consistent track record of success, other people's perception of my capability had shifted.

Towards the end of my pregnancy, it felt like people were just waiting for me to go. I didn't get invited to key meetings;

people stopped copying me into group emails. I was just an inconvenience. They recruited my maternity cover – a young, bright, very charming woman. She took over my projects, met my clients (who loved her), and off she went. On my last day, the team bought me a huge hamper and a lovely card. I was touched; they were all genuinely happy for me. I spent two weeks enjoying some downtime, had my baby, and didn't think any more of it. I moved on. I loved motherhood and maternity leave, and made a new group of friends in the mums and babies groups I went to.

Soon, the time to go back to work loomed over me. I wondered whether I should leave and start again somewhere else. I felt intimidated about going back into the office, slightly podgier, and sleep deprived. What if I couldn't do my job as well as I used to? What if my clients preferred my maternity cover? What if I couldn't do all the hours I used to? I was daunted by how people might respond to me. When the day came to meet my manager to discuss my return, I was nervous. For the first twenty minutes of the meeting, he was incredibly awkward with me. It was awful. I felt like the conversation was going in the wrong direction, and I could feel tears welling in my eyes. Eventually, he said, 'Emily, we desperately need you back. We miss your creativity and your insight, and the way you hold the whole team together. I'm sorry, I know I'm not allowed to put you under pressure, but I hope you're not here to tell me you're leaving.' And that was it – I burst into tears in his office. I just needed to hear that so much.

We planned my return. We agreed to a degree of flexibility so I could sort out nursery drop-offs and pick-ups; we talked about my concerns; and he reassured me completely. I wish I had spoken to him at the start of my pregnancy rather than assuming what everyone was thinking and feeling. On reflection, I also realised it was natural for people to start thinking about working without me – they had to. It wasn't necessarily malicious. I also realised that not every woman comes back to work to a supportive environment, and I felt lucky to have support at work to allow me to transition back and balance all the challenges that being a working mum brings."

A critical time for a woman is when they return to work after having a baby. Getting off to the right start is everything. You're tired, emotionally drained and you have to find new ways to do the most basic things, like getting ready to leave for work or making sure you have eaten!

Even though we might not want to admit it, having a baby has an impact on our careers, and it definitely has an impact on our earning potential. Women's earnings drop sharply after they have their first baby, and never recover. But this doesn't happen to men.[1] This is even the case in countries such as Denmark, which is well known for its relatively generous paid parental leave and subsidised childcare. Even if you have great childcare, it can be impossible to do all the discretionary things like business dinners and social events, and sometimes even the essential things, like the board meeting that runs over time.

In almost every country in the world, women earn less than men – in almost every type of work, and in almost every industry. In 2023, the average pay gap between men and women in EU countries was 12.7 per cent, with Luxembourg the only country to achieve gender pay parity.[2] In the UK, it was around 9 per cent.[3] But we are finally talking about it within organisations and governments, and this is driving action.

When I negotiate my pay now, I ask how I benchmark against my male peers, and I ask for confirmation of this from HR, not the person I am negotiating with. I don't need to know exactly what they earn; I just want to know I am in the same ballpark.

One of the leading thinkers on the gender pay gap is economist Claudia Goldin. Fittingly, when she won the Nobel Prize in Economics for her work on the topic, she was the first female winner not to have to share the prize with a man! Her work has shown that one of the main reasons for the gap is that women all over the world still do much more unpaid care work at home than men. Women disproportionately look for jobs that they can fit in around their commitments at home, whether this is in the form of flexible hours, less travel or working close to home, so they can leave early if necessary to handle emergencies. Many women take on the bulk of household chores during maternity leave, so childcare is often seen as being necessary to allow the woman to return to work, rather than enabling both parents to work. Men might need reminding that when their partner goes back to work after maternity leave, they need to think about what changes they can make to their working schedule so they can play an equal part in looking after the house and their family.

On 24 October 1975, 90 per cent of the women in Iceland, 25,000 of them, went on strike for a day to raise awareness about the gender pay gap, which at the time was 40 per cent.[4] Women took to the streets, not doing any work in the workplace or the home. They called this *kvennafri*, meaning 'day off'. The country came to a standstill: telephone switchboards went down, flights were cancelled and men had to take their children to work with them or stay at home. Soon afterwards, Iceland passed its first gender equality act and banned gender-based wage discrimination. Women's rights were added to the constitution and more women were elected to the government. Only five years later, the world's first democratically elected female president, Vigdís Finnbogadóttir, came to power in Iceland.

Almost fifty years later, the women of Iceland took *kvennafrí* again. On 26 October 2023 women all across the country, including Prime Minister Katrín Jakobsdóttir, took a day off all work – including unpaid work in the home – and marched for gender equality, under the banner of 'Call this Equality?' They called attention to the fact that their country was not upholding the standards the rest of the world had come to know it for. Importantly, they made the link between sexual violence, women's status in society and the monetary value associated with women's contribution. The women who organised the strike said: 'We are connecting the dots; violence against women and undervalued work of women in the labour market are two sides of the same coin and have an influence on each other.'

But, if you read some of the personal accounts of women involved in this inspiring movement, you will see something depressing. They talked about 'getting things prepared' in the days before the walk out, to make the day easier for men. Even the prime minister tried to discourage this by publicly stating, 'For one day it's not our problem, so let's not try to make it easier for them!' But as these women were making a groundbreaking statement to the whole world about women being undervalued, they still made packed lunches and laid clothes out for their children, so the men didn't have to.

---

1. *The Conversation*: (Article, 2024) The motherhood pay gap: why women's earnings decline after having children.
2. Eurostat: (Dataset, 2024) Gender pay gap in unadjusted form.
3. World Economic Forum: (Report, 2023) Global gender pay gap report 2023.
4. *The Women's History Archives*: (Article, 2023) Women's day off 1975.

Chapter Fifteen
Find a balance that works for you

Kerry is forty-two and lives in Somerset with her husband and two children. Kerry works in insurance and supports a local charity.

"*A few years ago, I had a big presentation to deliver to the chief exec of the business I worked for. I hadn't been there long and the project I had been delivering was high profile. This was my chance to demonstrate the work I had done. The meeting was at our head office in London and I had prepared for weeks. The CEO was old school. His board was made up of men, and the culture they had built was one of fear and intimidation. How these meetings went became a big part of whether you were successful or not in the company – they were like a test. They were also quite binary – if you did well, you were on the list. If you didn't, you weren't. But I was ready: my slides were clear and slick, my message was well rehearsed, and my thinking was insightful and on point. I had even bought a new blouse so I could feel brilliant walking into the lions' den. My boss was going to be there too – and he had helped coach me. My partner was working away, but I had booked my daughter into nursery early to allow me to get the train to London and be there in plenty of time to get a coffee and relax before the meeting.*

The night before, my daughter didn't have much of an appetite. She had a slight temperature and was unusually quiet and tired. She went to bed early and without any drama, which in hindsight should have raised the alarm.

About 2 a.m., I awoke to the sound of her vomiting in her bed. I ran into her bedroom and followed the usual middle-of-the-night sick child routine that all parents will be familiar with. I cleaned her up, and her bedroom, comforted her and got her back into bed, but we were in for a night of it. She threw up five more times that night and finally fell back to sleep in my bed at about 5 a.m. I sat on my bed, knowing I was done for. With my partner away and no family nearby, there was no way I could make the meeting. In the morning, I phoned my boss and explained that I couldn't make it. He tried to hide his disappointment, but I could hear it in his voice. I felt awful. I looked awful! I was exhausted, and gutted. In my exhausted state, the voice in my head told me it was career suicide, and I would never recover. My daughter woke up at about 8 a.m., right as rain. She ate two bowls of porridge for breakfast and wanted to go to the park, excited that she was getting to spend the day with me. I couldn't help feeling a little resentful. I had worked so hard, and now my boss was going to deliver the presentation as his work.

And what happened? My boss took total credit for all the work I had done. All this did, in my mind, was reinforce the macho culture of the organisation. I could almost hear the board's judgement as he explained I had to be home with my sick child – or maybe he didn't even mention me at all. Not long after this, I left the company but, even now, every time my kids go to bed early and with no drama, I start thinking about back-up childcare!"

It always makes me smile when people ask how I balance my responsibilities as a mother with the demands of my career. Depending on the person, I sometimes ask them if they would ask a man the same question. I usually don't, though, because it often comes from a woman in my network, just seeking support. The truth is, I constantly feel like I need to be in two places at once, and that I'm doing both things badly! I can't do every meeting, I leave the office early, I miss some school stuff, sometimes it's sandwiches for dinner. Some days it's a mess!

Luckily, most corporate environments are waking up to the importance of flexibility, for the most part. But there's a limit. People do understand the odd childcare emergency but, if it becomes a regular thing, they don't. And sometimes missing an important meeting because your kid has chicken pox means you miss out on an opportunity to get the credit for your brilliant work or influence something that's important to you. Outside the corporate environment, if you work in education, healthcare, retail, or work shifts, it can be almost impossible to get the flexibility you need to attend all the things.

The school system doesn't help. It is still largely designed for families with mothers at home, with the school day starting at nine and finishing at three. School performances and events around Christmas time or at the end of the school year lead to complex rescheduling of working parents' diaries and trading of who goes to what. Parents' "evening" offers appointments between 3 p.m. and 6 p.m. That's *not* the evening. That's the middle of my working day.

I think teachers do a fabulous job – I wouldn't want to do it. But I forget my gratitude towards them every year on the last day of school before the summer holidays. Our kids' school have an end-of-term family picnic (at 1.30 p.m., requiring a half day's annual leave), and all the teachers smile excitedly and say, 'Have a lovely summer!' I know, like me, most parents are entering the summer holiday period feeling dread, guilt and worry. Either they are working and navigating childcare and kids clubs, or they are reducing their working hours and compromising their financial security. I normally just reply 'You too', through gritted teeth!

From my own experience and from working with some amazing women, I have some tips:

Set your boundaries and stick to them

Work out what's important to you. For me, it's getting home for tea. I might not always make it, but I structure my day around trying to. For a friend of mine, it's doing the school run three days a week, so she structures her work around that. There will be compromises, of course there will. But if you are clear about what you're willing to compromise on, and what you're not, you'll be more able to get a balance you can live with. Be open about your needs with your colleagues, your manager, and your team. I never duck out of something for a vague reason – I say I'm working from home so I can do the school run. I encourage my team to do the same thing.

Organise good, reliable childcare you can trust

When I was pregnant with my daughter, I researched nurseries ruthlessly. I picked one that was staffed with people *I* wanted to spend time with, and when I went back to work, I knew my daughter was with good people. I was devastated when we moved and I had to find somewhere new for her. Unfortunately, all the nurseries where we were moving were oversubscribed – apart from one. I went to visit and I wasn't thrilled with it, but I needed childcare so I signed her up. But every day I cried on the way to work. I just knew it wasn't right. One day I picked her up and she had her shoes on the wrong feet and her clothes were wet. I knew I couldn't live like this, so I begged another local nursery that I loved to find a place for her. A couple of weeks later, they did, and I had peace of mind again.

Get all the help you can

If you can afford someone to clean your house, do it. If you can afford a nanny who can cook dinner every night, do it. Don't let that little voice in your head tell you it's outsourcing motherhood; it's not. That's not possible. But if, once you and your partner have done all you can, there are still gaps, then fill them with help. If, like us, you don't have family nearby, then get paid help, even if this soaks up a good proportion of your income. I have heard women say it's pointless going back to work because the entire additional family income is swallowed up by childcare costs. The thing is, it won't be forever! Eventually, your kids will be at school and the cost will reduce significantly. Not long after that, they will be at senior school and you won't need paid childcare. And by then you will have years of experience and salary growth under your belt. As much as it hurts, use your hard-earned income to fund the help you need, at the time in your life when you need it most.

Enjoy it!

On some days, when I come home from a stressful day at work to a messy kitchen, grumpy kids with homework still to do, and emails still pinging in, this advice feels ridiculous. On other days, I come home energised and fulfilled after a brilliant day at work, and then hug my kids and snuggle up in bed with them. These are my favourite days. I think: 'I got to do it all today. I might not have done it all to the standard I wanted to, or as well as someone else did, but I did it all.' What a buzz!

Chapter Sixteen
When your worlds collide

Sarah is a thirty-two-year-old mum of two children aged two and three months. Originally from Northern Ireland, she lives with her husband and children in West Sussex and works in the headquarters of a global defence company.

"In early 2021, I found out I was pregnant with my first baby. It was super exciting and, without knowing the protocol for not telling people you were pregnant in advance of the twelve-week scan, I freely told my colleagues and manager that I was going to have a baby.

At my twelve-week scan, I learned that the baby had no heartbeat and that I had unfortunately suffered a miscarriage.

I then went on to have about three months of complications, which were physically and mentally exhausting. It sounds bizarre, but at the time I dreaded telling my colleagues at work, who were all men. I was concerned about how awkward it would make them feel, or that they might feel they had to react in a certain way.

Twice through this experience there were times I wanted the ground to swallow me up. The first was with one of the senior executive directors. I was on a video call with my manager (who was absolutely incredible about the situation), talking about me taking on a new role, and this director had come into his office. He saw me on the screen and said, 'Oh, Sarah, hi! I hear congratulations are in order.' I automatically assumed he was talking about my pregnancy, so I responded, 'Oh, I'm not actually pregnant anymore, it didn't work out.' What I hadn't realised was that he was congratulating me on my new role. I was mortified – so mortified I emailed to apologise to him for putting him in an uncomfortable situation.

The second time was with an older male HR director, who on a call commented that I must be getting big now. I felt guilty that I had to say I wasn't actually pregnant anymore. He was deeply uncomfortable – and all I thought about was his feelings and how I had made him feel. He just changed the subject and we moved on. I hated it.

I hated myself for feeling responsible for ensuring that my colleagues weren't experiencing any discomfort at what I was telling them, instead of focusing on myself and allowing myself to be open and honest about my own feelings. Statistically, one in four pregnancies ends in miscarriage. These types of conversation are going to become more and more common as female representation increases in our workforce; we're going to have to get used to being comfortable with being uncomfortable. Conversely, was it unfair of me to downplay my emotions? Should I have shown how I felt, given my colleagues more credit?

I clearly didn't learn my lesson, because when I unexpectedly got pregnant for the third time, having had a baby after my miscarriage, I spent time apologising to colleagues because I had "promised" I would be focused on a new role for the next few years. I apologised to everyone, downplayed my pregnancy so much that, when I had a threatened miscarriage, I felt devastated – as if I had brought it upon myself. I have taken a step back from opportunities because of my pregnancy. I still don't know why – I felt like I was doing the business a favour by not going for something that I knew was business critical, when I should have pushed harder. I should have emphasised that promoting someone who was pregnant and about to go on maternity leave would show how far the company had progressed, and that pregnancy shouldn't be seen as a career blocker.

I've learned a lot through my pregnancy journeys with my company. I believe that, as a male-dominated industry, we can do better. I also think that women need to be easier on ourselves. We shouldn't have to hide our feelings out of fear of being labelled in a particular way, or to protect our colleagues from awkward situations. We should also continue to pursue opportunities without thinking we're doing the company a favour by stepping back."

As much as we might like to, we can't keep our work and home lives separate. We are one person. Our lives are messy, ugly and complex. We get divorced, have vomiting bugs and make mistakes. Trying to compartmentalise our lives into boxes will only make us miserable.

It's easy to feel like an inconvenience when personal things encroach on your work, especially when they involve something taboo like miscarriage. It takes bravery and strength to confront something like this at work and to talk openly about it. The thing is, you never know who you're helping when you do. Your mortifying moment could be the thing that encourages someone else to show vulnerability or talk about something they are struggling with.

For too long, being emotional at work has been seen as a negative thing, but this is deeply unhelpful and I think it gets in the way of us performing at our best. When I am leading a team, I encourage people to be open and vulnerable. I pull my team together regularly to talk about how we are feeling, what's going on for us, and how we can support each other. When I take on a new team, it can be difficult for people to get used to my insistence that we talk about our feelings. I recently led a large team of mainly men, including a couple of ex-army officers and engineers. When I first started asking them to talk about how they were feeling, in a team meeting, they felt pretty uncomfortable. Over time they got more comfortable with it, and they ended up being really open with the rest of the team about what was going on for them, at work and personally. Together, over months and years, we built a brilliant team environment. We could challenge each other, spot when someone wasn't at their best, and have arguments and get over them. Not only did we do some amazing things together, being part of it was fun. It felt a bit like family.

Part 3 – Community

Chapter Seventeen
The war on women

> Trigger warning – the following story contains a graphic description of sexual violence.

Emma is forty-three and lives in Hampshire. She works in engineering and lives with her husband and two young children.

"*I*n 1999, when I was eighteen, I went away to Leeds University. My childhood and adolescent years had been fairly lovely, and it was a super exciting time in my life. I remember being dropped off at the halls of residence by my parents who, having not been to university themselves, were a little bemused by the set-up. I had been placed on a floor of the halls that only had six rooms – a girl-only floor – and quickly made friends with the other five girls. We were all very different, and it's fair to say we never bonded as a group, each *of us finding our people in other areas of university life, either in clubs or the faculties we were a part of. One grim week in early November we all had colds and spent a few days together in our rooms, taking it in turns to bring each other tea and food. When we were all recovering, we decided to go out for the evening to a club – a grotty, smelly, sticky-floored nightclub of the early noughties, where we'd drink brightly coloured "cocktails" for £1 and shots in plastic shot glasses from a sticky tray.*

I wasn't out for long, but the combination of still being a little unwell, taking cold medicine and a few drinks under my belt had made me feel pretty rubbish, so I told the others I was going to go back to the halls and go to bed. I jumped in a taxi and went back and got into bed. Later that night, I heard the others come back. I could hear male voices – they had brought some guys back. Someone knocked loudly on my door as they walked past, and everyone laughed. I just turned over and tried to go back to sleep. Shortly after, the noise died down, and it seemed as if everyone had left or gone to bed. Then I heard my door handle turn, and realised I hadn't locked it. It was pitch black, but I felt someone cross the room quickly, put one hand on my shoulder and pull the covers down. Faster than I thought possible, they had pulled my underwear to one side and entered me, one arm across my chest, pinning me against the bed, and the other pushing themselves inside me. He made a 'shhh' sound. In the darkness, I could just about make out his face as he looked down at me. I didn't shout, or scream, or even fight; I just froze. When he was done, he lifted himself off me, stood up and left. I heard him swear as he left, seemingly angry about something, and heard him zip his trousers up. As the door clicked shut, I just lay there in the darkness. I didn't know what to do.

After what seemed like hours, but was probably minutes, I reached over and turned my bedside lamp on. I looked down at my bed and saw blood everywhere. I was covered in blood from my waist to my knees. The sudden, unwanted penetration had torn me inside. This had clearly been the cause of his frustration; he must have been covered in blood too. Immediately wanting to erase what had just happened, I very calmly got out of bed, went to the communal showers and cleaned myself thoroughly. I stripped my bed and replaced the bedding. I scrubbed the patch of smeared blood that was on my carpet. By this time the sun was coming up, I got back into bed and lay there, completely numb.

Later that morning, the girl who had the room adjacent to mine knocked on my door. She came in with a cheeky smile. 'Sounds like someone got lucky last night?'

I burst into tears. She looked around and saw the bloodstained bedding, the patch of blood that I couldn't get out of the carpet. I told her what had happened, and she immediately phoned the university helpline, who sent the welfare officer round to see me. At this point, it felt like everything was taken out of my hands. I was taken to a clinic, given the morning-after pill, swabbed for sexually transmitted infections (STIs) (having my feet in stirrups mere hours after having been raped was one of the darkest moments of my life), given a blood test for HIV and told I'd have to come back for more tests six weeks later. I then found myself being interviewed by a female police officer in a cold, sterile office on the university campus. She looked at me with a rehearsed kindness and asked me lots of questions. She asked me to describe what had happened in as much detail as I could, and probed and prodded for every little detail. Why had I come home early without my friends? What time had I come home? What time had my friends come home? Did I know the group of guys they had brought home? Did I see or hear them say or do anything? What time did he come into my room? Why hadn't I locked my door? What did he look like? Smell like? Sound like? Did he have a beard? Any piercings? What colour was his hair? How tall was he? Did he say anything? Did I call for help? Had I tried to fight him? Why not? Did he ejaculate inside me? Was I sure I hadn't been on my period, and that was what had caused all the bleeding? Why had I showered straight afterwards and cleaned my room? Why hadn't I locked my door? And again ... why hadn't I locked my door? The interview took over an hour and it felt more invasive than anything I had ever experienced, apart from the rape itself.

She then explained that because I didn't know anything about him or who he was, it was very unlikely they would find him without significant investigative resource (the subtext being they would not spend this level of resource) interviewing lots of people at the university, starting with the girls I lived with (imagine the shame). If they did identify him, and if the Crown Prosecution Service (CPS) decided it was 'worth pursuing', they would open a case. They would then examine my entire sexual history, read my phone records and messages, and interview my friends and family to find out whether I was a reliable, believable witness. However, they would not be allowed to investigate his sexual history and, even if he had raped a woman before, they would not be allowed to present this as evidence because it would be deemed prejudicial to my case. She was clear that it would be a bruising process for me, and that the chance of a prosecution was very low. Looking back now, I'm not sure whether she was quite as blunt as this, but this is my recollection of the conversation. I told her I didn't want that. She gave me a kind but rather patronising smile, closed her notebook and left.

The day after that, I went to the office and asked the university if I could change rooms. They said unfortunately they were full that year, and I'd have to wait until the following September.

I went back to my room and got on with my life. I never told anyone about what had happened, and the friend who had found me never mentioned it again. I had gone back to the halls without my friends, I hadn't locked my door, I had cleaned up straight afterwards, and I hadn't fought him. I didn't even call for help.

I tried to put it behind me. I pushed my bedside table in front of my door every night and tried to stay awake as long as possible because, every time I started falling asleep, I would hear the door handle click. I started drinking every day, regularly drinking myself into oblivion, and started skipping lectures. By Christmas, I was so far behind, I quit my course and went home. Unable to move back in with my family, I stayed with a friend and hid myself away for the next few years. I enrolled in the same course at the university in my hometown and restarted my degree, but I opted out of university life. I didn't go to a single bar, nightclub, party or social gathering for the next three years. I attended my lectures, studied in the library, worked a part-time job and went home. I had no friends. But I graduated with a First and went on to have a fantastic life and wonderful career.

When I look back now, I wonder what my university experience would have been like if I hadn't been raped, and I feel cheated. I have friends who talk with such fondness about their days as a student: the hobbies they picked up, the friends they made, who are now godparents to their children, and the lifelong memories of being young and carefree. I feel sad for the young girl who was caught up in a system that wasn't able to respond to what happened to her. I wish I could go back and tell her that everything would be OK. That it wasn't her fault, and that she did nothing wrong. Forgetting to lock her door, not fighting him off, cleaning herself up in an attempt to get rid of the horrific trauma of what had just happened to her: none of those things justified what he did or made it her fault. I sometimes wonder who he was and whether he remembers it. I hope the next girl he tried to rape stabbed him in the heart. I wish I had done that.

The first time I told someone what had happened, years later, she told me she had been raped by a male friend who wouldn't take no for an answer. Another friend told me she had been abused by an uncle. Another friend was sexually assaulted by her boss on a work night out. It happens to so many women; it's shockingly common."

Women and girls are subject to obscene rates of sexual violence every day, all over the world. The statistics are shocking, depressing and anger inducing. It seems like we are so far away from living in a world where women and girls can live their lives in safety.

In England and Wales, one in four women have been raped or sexually assaulted as an adult. That's 6.5 million women. Like in Emma's case, one in three rapes happen in a woman's own home.[1] One in three.

Since 2016, there has been a devastating decline in rape prosecutions, partly because The Crown Prosecution Service decided to cut the number of rape cases it prosecuted to hit a target conviction rate of 60 per cent. Within a year of this decision, 1,000 fewer rapes were being investigated and, within two years, 2,000 fewer.[2] Without a prosecution there can be no conviction, and so rape convictions have been at their lowest rate for years. For the women who do persevere to trial, a rape case can take three years for the trial to happen, and most trial dates are set, cancelled and rescheduled multiple times. The experience of giving evidence is often described as more traumatic than the rape itself. In the last few years, rape survivors in the UK have been able to give evidence for the trial via pre-recording, but the data shows these cases have a lower conviction rate in court.

Women who speak up about all forms of sexual violence are still subject to intense shaming, gaslighting and persecution by the very system that is supposed to protect them. The most shocking part of the current process in the UK is the so-called 'digital strip search' that victims of rape have to suffer if they find the courage to report the offence to the police. When they make a complaint, they are requested to immediately hand over their mobile phone, which is then scrutinised in detail. Specialist advisers report that, when victims decline to do this, it routinely results in immediate closure of the investigation. A victim's credibility is examined and judged in rape cases more intensely and more harshly than in any other type of crime. Rape victims are also subject to searches of "third-party materials", meaning any data about them in the hands of third parties, including medical and therapeutic records, educational data and social services records, with the sole purpose of undermining their credibility. We hear so much about the culture of misogyny and prejudice in police forces around our country – right from the start the system is against us.

We'll probably never understand the true scale of violence against women and girls globally, particularly in the case of intimate partner violence, because social pressure in many parts of the world makes it impossible for women to report it. The statistics we do have are shocking. Globally, 26 per cent of women (aged fifteen and older) have been subject to some form of physical or sexual violence at the hands of their partner, with adolescent girls particularly at risk.[3][4] In countries such as Guinea and Mali, 75 per cent of the population think it is acceptable to beat your wife if she burns your food or doesn't keep the house tidy enough – and this includes women! Women and girls all over the world are raped and then blamed for it. In some countries, they are killed for having sex outside marriage, even when the sex is violent and against their will.

Girls as young as five suffer female genital mutilation (FGM) at the hands of their older, often female, relatives, often without pain relief or anaesthetic, to make them "purer" and more attractive to the men in their community. "Virginity testing" was only made illegal in the UK in 2022, when the Department of Health and Social Care recognised it as a form of violence against women and girls. Women and girls are trafficked and hidden from our view to be used for sexual gratification and profiteering. And it's not just in far-flung places across the world; it happens here in the UK, right in front of us.

It's hard to overstate how isolated a woman can feel as a result of violence or abuse. It's time we started amplifying the voices of these women and talking about these issues with solutions in mind.

The appalling treatment of women and girls all over the world affects us all. It perpetuates the power imbalance between the sexes and normalises victimisation. It ripples through our society, in the porn our teenagers watch on their phones, in the male patient who thinks it's OK to put his hand on the female doctor's leg, in the teenager who can't take being rejected by the girl he fancies and calls her a slut.

We need to keep talking about it and my view is that, if you are not part of the solution, you are part of the problem. Our boys and girls need to be educated about consent, respect and relationships from the start – and we adults need to role-model the right values and behaviours. The men in our lives need to stand beside us and call it out when they see signs of unacceptable behaviour from other men, before it escalates into something more serious.

These things that happen to women are not remote. They impact all of us and we need to drive change from every angle. Most importantly, we need to strengthen support networks for victims of sexual violence, and prioritise safe spaces for women to heal and feel less alone.

---

1. Rape Crisis: (Article, 2024) Rape and sexual assault statistics.

2. Victims Commissioner: (Report, 2021) The distressing truth is that if you are raped in Britain today, your chances of seeing justice are slim.

3. Office for National Statistics (Dataset, 2023): Sexual offences prevalence and victim characteristics, England and Wales

4. World Bank Group: (Article, 2022) Violence against women and girls – what the data tell us.

Chapter Eighteen

The cultural context

Jax is a single mum to five adult children. She navigates work and life between Cambridge and Sydney and everywhere in between. She has worked over four continents for three decades in financial services, and now runs her own successful business coaching and change company.

"*I've had an international life and have worked in nineteen countries. I understand that working in places and travelling through doesn't mean that you're part of the culture, but what it did for me was make me curious about how things work and how cultural systems operate.*

I grew up in Australia, in a culture that was still very old-fashioned: women stayed at home and put dinner on the table for their husbands. It was quite a challenging upbringing, and I got married at just twenty-one. My husband was a Pacific Islander. We moved to the island of Tonga, and for me it felt like going home.

I found myself in a culture where people support each other, and it taught me so much about what we're missing in Western culture. Everyone is interested in, and works together on, what happens in their village. If you see someone looking unhappy, you ask them in for tea. There's a real sense of community, and it's largely underpinned by the women.

In the Pacific Islands, and specifically in Tonga, women hold the mana, *or the power. Women are the head of the household, and they have an important role in society. The eldest sister of the oldest man in the family is the matriarch, the guru, the boss. She calls the shots in the family: she organises family events such as weddings and funerals. She names all the children in the family. She calls a family meeting when there's any drama.*

In Tonga, people also have a different approach to beauty standards. They don't care about whether you have a cute nose or whether you're a size six. Beauty standards are more about how you present yourself within the construct of the Tongan culture, which is centred around respect, humility, cultivating healthy relationships, and loyalty. Physical appearance doesn't come into it, with the exception of hair, which is very important from a spiritual point of view.

The women in Tonga come together to make things. They are the makers, and they are proud to be the makers. In our society, we are ashamed to be the makers or to be the one who stays at home. They make all sorts of handicrafts, such as tapa, *which is bark tapped out into a cloth-like product and decorated with patterns. It is highly valued and used for special occasions, but also put to more practical uses, as bedcovers and room dividers.*

The women are not making tapa for tourists to buy at the airport; they make it for themselves or for family members. They might spend weeks, even months, making tapa *because they – or someone they know – have a daughter who's getting married, or a big event is happening. Everybody comes together to make what you need. There are no complaints, no whining, no one saying, 'Oh, I don't feel well' or 'I can't be bothered'. They want to make it for you, and you know that sooner or later you will be making it for someone else. There's a feeling that you never really own anything because everything is 'ours'. It even goes as far as children. Your auntie is your mother; your cousins are your siblings. In Western culture, we have a lot of selfishness, even among siblings or neighbours; people feeling like 'this is mine'. But in the grand scheme of life, we don't own anything. Instead, we get our power from helping others – our network, our family, our friends.*

When I first arrived in Tonga, they treated me with huge respect. At first it was embarrassing because they were incredibly welcoming. They would bring me a chair when everyone else would sit on the floor, or they would drink homemade lemonade but bring me a can of soda. I knew I wasn't going to fully integrate into the society unless I could speak the language, because even the Tongans who could speak English would never speak English to another Tongan, so I made a conscious effort to learn the language, and now I speak fluent Tongan.

And that was also how I got into banking. What I really wanted to do was to support these women's groups, to support their communities and their families financially but, in those days, microfinance wasn't accessible. I set about getting to know and spend time with these groups and, through the bank I worked for, I managed to arrange a set of finance structures that allowed them to borrow small amounts of money, collectively. This was a big deal in the banking organisation, which had big reservations – 'What if they don't pay it back? It's a big group of people, who do we go after?'. I needed to find a solution to these reservations, a solution that would work in that environment, so I went to speak to the village chief. What I realised was that the women would always pay the chief back, and this was the reassuring protection that unlocked the opportunity.

What my time there gave me, and what I have taken with me all around the world, is a feeling of not being selfish and working together. Even though I don't live in Tonga anymore, I use everything I learned there in how I operate today, both at work and at home.

I left Tonga as I wanted my girls to be educated overseas, so we moved back to Australia, where I had three more children. I then started travelling for various jobs for the bank and ended up running the Pacific region, looking after eleven countries, including Fiji, Guam and Samoa, and then went on for assignments in Asia including working and living in Malaysia, and the Philippines.

In 2006, I worked in Papua New Guinea, which has a very different, but very interesting, culture. It's quite a challenging country to work in: there are 800 or so different tribes, and around 80 per cent of the population are illiterate. There were issues with domestic violence; it was heartbreaking to see many women in the team engaged in abusive relationships. I found that a lot of women at work were being hurt by the men in their lives: their boyfriends, their husbands, sometimes their fathers. It was very difficult for them to get to safety. I worked with an awesome group of women there, and we decided to get all the at-risk women who worked for us a pink phone. In that culture, men would never be seen with anything that was pink, so the women all got a pink phone with 'Mary' written on it, which means 'woman'. We knew that nobody would steal their phones. We then created a series of safe houses.

In Papua New Guinea, there's a lot of money from oil and gas, but not a lot of money gets distributed among the people. A lot of men work in the mines, but they were spending the money they earned and little of it was getting back to their wives and children. I wondered how to support the women and children at home, often in remote villages. I looked at what was happening in Kenya: there, women had a mobile wallet. In those days, we didn't have mobile banking, but in Kenya they were pioneering this technology where people could keep money stored on their phone. Over time, I did a deal with the telecommunications company and, with the use of a platform that was developed in Cambridge, we developed a mobile wallet. The next problem was, how would I get people to use money on a phone if they can't read and write? I ended up getting funding from the UN and, using my experience from Tonga, we trained all the village chiefs in how to use the phones, using pictures.

We ended up with an infrastructure where the mines would pay the miners and money would go on the phone, and then they would transfer a certain amount to their wife back in the village. She would then be able to go into the local shop and buy food and anything else she needed, so the shopkeepers were happy too.

I learned that you've got to work with the system. It's not for me to change the culture in another country. I am a guest in that country, and the opportunity to learn was epic. Get to understand the people, the traditions, the values, the environment, the elders – all these things hold such treasure and teach us all so much about ourselves."

Culture doesn't just emerge at a national level, country by country; it develops within companies, organisations, even individual teams. It's the social glue that holds people together, and it guides how we think, behave, communicate and make decisions. It also underpins our biases and expectations. It determines whether we think it's OK to beat each other, whether girls study maths, whether women are spoken down to in a car showroom. It affects how we see and interact with each other, and even how we see ourselves.

What Jax learned while travelling the world and working in different cultures was that, as much as we might want to, we can't change a culture single-handed – it takes critical mass and time. But what we can do is work with the system to do good and live by our own values.

I once came across a young female engineer who was working in an all-male operational environment. The way the men treated her was abhorrent. She was effectively being sexually harassed by her manager and, when she complained about it, the system failed to protect her. Instead, it protected him, and she was forced to leave the job she loved and take up a different role, which was office based. When I met her, she was facing an impossible situation – get off the career path she loved and had worked hard to achieve, or work in this culture, which was damaging her. Listening to her made me angry. I badly wanted to go down there and fix the toxic culture. But I couldn't. It was so ingrained and went back so far. Those people had been working in that environment, in that way and with those views, for so long that, no matter how wrong it was, I couldn't fix it. But I could be an ally for her. I could support her and help her see that she wasn't the one in the wrong here, but that the organisation had let her down. I helped her navigate the business and make new contacts, and soon she was promoted into a different part of the business where she could thrive.

Even if you're not in charge, you have the power to change the culture around you, bit by bit. Being in a position of influence isn't the only way to make a difference – by consistently showing up with the right behaviours and leading by example, you can inspire other people around you to speak up and change things. It doesn't happen overnight, but if you're willing to stand up for what you believe in, you can make others take notice. You might not even realise you've done it. I wonder how many people working alongside Jax were inspired to do something against the grain because they saw her do it. I feel sure my engineer colleague will pay forward the support she got, and support someone else. And that's what changes the world.

Chapter Nineteen

Resist the pressure to conform

Liz is forty-two and lives in Wiltshire with her husband Aaron. She works as a senior leader in the aviation industry.

"*I was lucky to have great parents. I had a hard-working mum and was lucky to have both my dad and stepdad, who were amazing. My parents worked a lot and weren't home until nearly seven every night. My brother and I would get home from school and do things like cook dinner and walk the dog and do some chores. We became very independent, very young. I was in a very equitable environment growing up and saw professional success as a key part of my future. Through my education, joining the Navy and then working in professional roles, I have watched others change their career path after they had children, and I always wondered what this would mean for me.*

When I met my husband, he didn't really care about having kids. If I'd wanted them, he would have had them, but he was easy either way. It was liberating that the choice was completely mine. I decided that I wanted to focus on my career and the satisfaction I got from being successful professionally. I felt that having children would be too much of a compromise for me. What would be the purpose of having children, other than to tick a box? Would it change what I wanted to do? Would it restrict me?

Some people in our lives struggled with our decision. I was in my late twenties when we got married. Every time I saw friends, they asked when we were having a baby, which became quite frustrating. I'm stubborn, too. When people pushed me, it made me pull away from the idea even more, because I felt like I was being pressurised into it. It was expected that having children was the next logical step after getting married.

Maybe some people would call me selfish for believing that my work is more important to me than having children but, in my thirties, I just became more comfortable with myself. I was comfortable in my routine, I knew what I liked and what I wanted, and I loved my life. I loved having my own time at the weekends and going on holiday during term time. It became more and more of a positive choice to say no, and my thirties solidified that for me.

For the most part, people have stopped asking me, but the societal pressures are still there. My mum has said a few times that she hopes I won't regret not having children. But I don't believe in regret; I positively made this choice and I'm happy with it. I can see why people get a lot of joy from children – I have two nephews and I love them to pieces. But I can do the things I want to do without feeling guilty or pressured. My mum also says she wishes I'd had children because my brother's wife goes to her mum with child-related problems or for advice. She sees their relationship and wishes I could lean on her in the same way. But I remind her that she brought me up to be independent. I've made my choice, and I respect the choice of others, but the world doesn't need everyone to have children!

We're living in a time where women can make different choices. Of course, we can have a family and a career if we want to, but then there are compromises, and I don't want to compromise. I also think that not having children has allowed me to invest in my relationship with my husband. He's my best friend, he's everything to me, and we do everything together. I see other couples we know and see that all their energy goes into the kids; the relationship comes second. But our relationship works brilliantly because we're focused on each other. I wonder how it would have been if we'd had kids –

especially because he wasn't desperate to have kids. I know that if I had wanted them, or had got pregnant, he would have been great. But I do wonder whether it would have affected our relationship.

I don't have any regrets. I always try to look forward, and I love my life. I love our luxurious travel and the fact I can drive a two-seater car! I can be totally selfish, other than considering my husband, without guilt or pressure. I don't feel guilty if I work late, although my husband will make sure I don't work too long or too hard! I think this approach means I don't feel obliged to do things just because of societal pressure. I've only got one life and I will live it the way I want to. We should all be free to make choices that make us love our lives, and not make excuses for our choices, no matter what other people think."

There's still so much pressure on us to conform to what society expects from us. It's instilled in us from a very young age. It takes strength, courage and the will to be different to go against the grain. There's so much pressure on women to have babies, partly because the window of opportunity is finite. The choice not to have children can also be controversial because of the impact it has on others – potential grandparents or aunts and uncles.

But I think we are seeing a generational shift in women's ability and willingness to say no to things, generally. It's something I teach my daughter very deliberately – it's OK to say no. Unfortunately, that often gets thrown back at me when I want her to clean her room! But I hope that one day she will have the courage, like Liz, to say 'No, I don't want to', and to feel confident and positive about her choices.

Three years ago, I made the choice to stop drinking alcohol. It was a positive and empowering choice for me, and something I benefit from every day. Yet people still question me. They want to know why. I've even had people encourage me to 'just have one', and act amazed at the idea of me not having a drink on my birthday, or on Christmas Day, or at a wedding. I even did karaoke on a work night out completely sober. Not drinking alcohol is oddly controversial! People think surely you can't possibly have as much fun. They might think I'm boring or a secret alcoholic. I've had plenty of people ask me if I'm pregnant! But I just don't want to, and that should be enough.

I think we need to build stronger communities where we support each other's choices, not criticise them. We need to lift each other up instead of tearing each other down. The supportive atmosphere women can create for each other should form a buffer against the judgement of the world and support us to make the most of the freedom to choose, and the freedom to say 'No, I don't want to'.

Chapter Twenty

Don't let anything hold you back

Lou is a fifty-seven-year-old mother of one daughter (aged twenty-five). Lou lives in Hertfordshire with her second husband, who brought four amazing stepdaughters and eight step-grandchildren into Lou's life. Lou is co-director of Women in Change,[1] which unites women who lead change and drive impact in the world.

> *I went to school in the 1970s, and I really struggled. I was always bottom of the class, no matter what I did. I just couldn't grasp how people could pass exams. I couldn't scrape through even with the biggest of incentives! To boot, I had the*

cleverest brother in the world – a straight A student, creative, a linguist, there was nothing he couldn't do.

When I was fourteen or fifteen, my French teacher made me stand up in class and made everyone applaud. She said that I clearly did not have paralysis of the right arm because I had managed to pass my Latin exam. I was mortified. I can still imagine the scene: I know exactly where I was standing, with everyone laughing at me. I can still feel the trauma and humiliation to this day.

Not long before my O levels, I remember being taken to a test centre. They showed me flashcards and asked me about pictures of different items, but I didn't know what it was all about. A few weeks after that, I came home from school to find my mother crying. She said, 'You'd better sit down. We've had the most devastating news. They say you're dyslexic.' I didn't understand what it meant and nobody ever explained it to me. My mother concluded: 'Clearly you're never going to be anything or do anything with your life, because you can't read or write.' I was so confused… I could read and write! I just couldn't pass exams. She just kept saying my life was over.

In careers classes at school, they would ask me what I wanted to do, and I'd say I wanted to go into journalism. They all pretty much laughed at me – how can you go into journalism when you're dyslexic?!

After school, quite remarkably – since I failed most of my O levels – I was offered an apprenticeship scheme that the government had just started, called the Youth Training Scheme, at Marks & Spencer. They sent me to college, and I went on to pass a business degree. Everyone else on my course found it so hard. It was the first time I remember thinking, this is easy! I realised that, if something interested me, I could be good at it. I passed my degree, and Marks & Spencer thought I was fabulous! They put me on their management scheme, and within seven years I was a manager rolling out a new computerised system across London. I started to recognise that I had a superpower – the dyslexia meant I could see and explain things in ways that other people couldn't. I can work out puzzles. I'm the one who can see obstacles before they appear.

After that, my career went from strength to strength. I started to understand more about my dyslexia: that it helped me visualise things and find ways of exciting people. I excelled at challenging people and encouraging them to try something new. I went into a small business selling training resources to blue-chip companies, helping them to grow significantly, and when the owner decided he didn't need me anymore, I found an investor and went into competition with him. I set up in central London and, as I built my own business, I started to recognise that my core skill was to build things. I also realised I was good at public speaking. At school, my teachers laughed at me when I said I wanted to do anything that involved writing or words, but with the support of my amazing cousin, I found I can stand on stage and talk for hours – I don't need a script!

Later in my career, I was offered the role of head of production for a major national media company. I honestly didn't know how I could ever do that job! I've never held a camera; I've never made a programme. But he said, 'We've got all that. But what I haven't got is someone who knows how to do what you do.'

The job was extremely challenging. The production team weren't very happy to have me as their boss, and it wasn't great to join a media company, writing and developing materials, being dyslexic. I had to make sure I had the right support around me. I learned that the best teams are the ones that bring diverse people together and find a way to get the best out of them. After several successful roles, I was offered the role of head of internal communications – again, I had to pinch myself. A dyslexic person running the internal comms department! For the first time, I was honest about having a disability. I then went on to several brilliant roles and have many successes, including being content editor for a magazine.

And then things got tricky. We were running a project that everyone knew would fail, but nobody would listen to us. My boss didn't understand any form of neurodivergence and was the worst kind of female leader you could ever meet. Sadly, some of the people around her felt they had to behave like that too.

So far in my career, I'd never had any issues. I'd worked in big corporates, run my own business, I'd run vlogs, I'd been a storyteller, a programme maker – yet this woman was out to destroy me. Even after everything I had achieved, she still had the power to make me doubt my own ability. My work would come back with red pen all over it. I would be constantly shut down in meetings. I was ghosted. It was incredibly isolating.

Eventually, she started a process to manage me out of the business. I was called to a meeting with her and she refused to be in the room with me. I was taken to a room, just me and an 'Access to Work' woman who had been brought in as an independent person, and a phone. The woman and two other team members were on the line. I couldn't believe where I'd ended up. I'd worked since I was sixteen, and here I was, in my late forties, in this situation.

I was a bag of nerves – an absolute wreck. The Access to Work woman explained why we were there and asked my boss to give some examples of why she thought I couldn't do the job. She gave ridiculous examples, like me not being able to turn my work around quickly enough. The Access to Work woman basically shut her down. What my boss was describing in terms of her expectation would not have been reasonable even for someone without a disability. She explained: 'Your expectations of Lou, regardless of her disability, are unfair.' As we left the building, she gave me her card and said, 'When you go to the tribunal, which you're clearly going to have to because they are managing you out, please make sure I'm invited to testify against this woman. I will be there for you.' Luckily, it didn't get that far.

The experience took me right back to being fourteen, and it broke me. After everything I had been through, everything I had worked for, it took everything away from me. It destroyed my confidence, and I had to start all over again. With the support of my therapist, amazing husband and great friends, I was able to build myself back.

I'm now co-founder of an organisation called Women in Change, and we have almost 2,500 people involved so far. We have just launched our first Women in Change magazine, which went live in June 2024 and has reached over 100,000 people. So I find myself, again, doing the thing I dreamed of, that everyone told me I'd never achieve.

I wish I knew, growing up, that it was OK to dream big. We can all be whatever we want to be in life, no matter what other people tell us. We just have to be prepared to put in the hard work."

It doesn't take much to knock our self-belief. An ill-judged comment by a parent or teacher in childhood can plant a seed that can grow into a mighty oak of self-doubt that affects every decision we make throughout our lives. The problem is, women already have a psychological predisposition to doubt ourselves. If you ask a woman why she has been successful, she'll say she's been lucky, that she had good mentors, that someone took a chance on her. You'll rarely hear her say, 'Well, I'm really good at my job!'

We talk ourselves out of trying new things and taking new opportunities. We also have lower expectations for ourselves than men do. A Manchester Business School study in 2011 asked students approaching graduation what they expected to earn five years later. On average, the men thought they deserved 20 per cent more than the women. A study carried out in 2024,[2] which asked men and women to predict how well they would do at answering spatial awareness questions, saw women consistently underestimate their own ability. Gender was a stronger predictor of underestimation than personality.

This self-doubt has an impact on representation within leadership roles in organisations in all sectors. Rather than a 'glass ceiling', McKinsey[3] calls it the 'broken rung'

– women are held back at their first step up to a management position. For every 100 men promoted to entry-level management positions, only 87 women have the same opportunity, and we never catch up. The pool of women gaining experience and applying for senior roles gets smaller and smaller.

I've seen this myself when trying to recruit for senior roles. If I open a vacancy for a leadership role, I will get many excellent male candidates and, if I'm lucky, one or two women. Sometimes the female applicants are excellent, and sometimes they are outperformed by their male counterparts – that's the nature of competition – but if the pool is skewed to begin with, it's harder to achieve a balance.

Find a woman and support her. Be her mentor, her guide, her advocate. We need to be champions and flagbearers for each other, to speak up for each other and for ourselves. Amplify our voices. We need to recognise our own talent and abilities, and not be afraid to talk about them. It took me to be almost finished with writing this book to have the confidence to tell people I was writing it! More importantly, we need to reach into ourselves for confidence when making decisions and progressing our lives. We also need to recognise that all sorts of things can make us feel like we can't do something – but sometimes we just have to grit our teeth and do it anyway!

1. Women in Change: (Website, 2024) Uniting women leading change and driving impact in the world.

2. Sciety: (Study, 2024) Women's humility and men's lack of hubris: Gender biases in self-estimated spatial intelligence.

3. McKinsey & Company: (Report, 2023) Women in the workplace 2023.

Chapter Twenty-One
Think free

Laura is an Orthodox Jewish woman living in North London with her young family. She qualified as a chartered surveyor and now runs a department for a busy emergency service. Laura is the trustee of a charitable trust and is currently working towards a master's in existential coaching.

"*High standards can be interpreted differently by different people, and I often find myself navigating between very different meanings and definitions in my life. I am both a senior leader in my workplace and an Orthodox Jewish woman. In my role at work, I'm expected to deliver targets and solve problems. I lead teams and give direction. In my community, the role of women seems more traditional, however, there are some similarities as there are still high standards to meet.*

Every week there is the Sabbath to prepare for, and hosting many guests for the main meal is usual. Before festivals, there are rituals to complete, foods and clothes to prepare, and occasionally the need to pull off a full family fancy-dress theme. There is a continual need to plan ahead for my family and friends, and provide for those in need in the community – ensuring no one is excluded is considered a mitzvah (positive deed).

At the start of my career, balancing the distinct roles of my workplace and community while maintaining my sense of self-identity was a constant challenge. I used to maintain strict boundaries and felt that deviating from these could result in negative consequences for my family in the community or could start a dreaded 'difficult conversation' about religion in my workplace. This came to a head after the birth of my final baby, a third son. I felt alone and isolated at the thought of having no other women in my family. I felt that my faith meant I was supposed to be grateful to be a mother; that was the appropriate response to my new addition. I felt I had nowhere to turn to share my loneliness, while my sons and husband had a place and a role. I have since realised that I needed to mourn the loss of the daughter I would not have, to find a way forward. This is a lesson I continue to apply, understanding that even exciting new beginnings inevitably include endings.

Emerging from the hurt of my postnatal experience, I learned that pain and suffering don't always have to be linked. I still find many situations difficult. However, I now find beauty and value in my religion. It feels very special to know that the clothes I wear or the meal I prepare is for a greater purpose. The sense of my family belonging to a community is a reassuring privilege. My religion means we have a day without technology every week, and it teaches the kids to aim for their own high standards, which matches what I believe in.

There are only 16 million Jewish people worldwide. I feel the pressure of being part of a minority culture makes exceeding standards even more important to overcome discrimination and prejudice. However, I now feel empowered from the recognition of my skill in navigating two sets of opposing high standards. It shapes who I am. This was made very real for me last year when I arrived home just before sundown on a Friday night, having won a prestigious award at a ceremony in central London. My family seemed pleased, but their enthusiasm for the chicken soup I then placed on the table was much more tangible. And that's fine too. The award was for me; my soup was always intended for them."

We don't have to be just one person. We can move between multiple roles and personas and meet different needs and expectations in sometimes very different environments. I think this is an amazing skill that women develop from an early age. We are wives, mothers, executives, professionals, experts, leaders, doctors, teachers and a hundred other things all in one day. Making peace with, and even finding strength in, the transition from one persona to the next frees us from the mental friction that playing multiple different roles can create in our mind and in our soul.

Some people say that our role in society has changed, but what has actually happened is that we now have multiple simultaneous roles, each with different expectations. Sometimes, these different roles mean we have to act very differently to be considered successful in any of them. We have to switch hats from managing director to mother in the half-hour drive home.

Somehow, in this crazy, busy world where we are balancing priorities, spinning plates and playing our multiple roles, we have to find a way to maintain our sense of self, and not see our different roles as conflicting with each other. Taking pleasure in cooking for your family doesn't mean you are betraying your professional, independent self. Being a caring, loving partner and prioritising your husband's needs does not make you any less of a feminist.

For me, thinking free means finding ways to live our multiple identities, without losing our authenticity.

Chapter Twenty-Two

Pick your partner with care

Rebecca is forty-four and lives in Edinburgh with her ten-year-old son, Dylan. She runs her own business and is studying for a master's degree.

"My mum always said to me when I was younger that I should choose a partner who's thoughtful and kind, and I used to think that sounded really boring. But now at the grand old age of almost forty-five, I wish I'd listened to her.

When I was in my late twenties, I met a guy in a bar while having a drink with my friend. He was charming and good-looking – just my type. We had a great conversation, and he asked for my number. We started seeing each other, we'd stay round each other's houses, we met each other's friends *and family, and it was a bit of a whirlwind romance. Not long after we met, we got engaged, and then we were married, and I got pregnant with Dylan pretty much straight after the wedding. It all happened so fast.*

When Dylan arrived, I got a bit of a shock – I had to be a mother. But what shocked me even more was that my husband expected nothing to change. He still wanted to go out with his mates a couple of times a week. He also drank heavily, whereas I went the other way; I didn't want to drink when I had to get up and feed our baby every ten minutes.

When I went back to work, I was commuting to London. Every week I would do two long days in London, then two long days at home, and then I'd be off on Friday and go and do baby stuff. He had a shift job, and Dylan would often stay at my mum and dad's. What I found out later was that my husband had parties – I suspect now that he had lots of affairs. Things gradually got worse. We snapped at each other and argued a lot. He was unreliable.

When Dylan was two, I bought tickets to the theatre so we could see Postman Pat live. It was a bit of a risk – would he sit still long enough? He did well, but I clearly remember looking at my husband and thinking, 'You look like death. You look so hungover' and finding him deeply unattractive.

Not long after this, there was the moment that ended it all. I had a bad cold and I'd gone up to bed early. He'd slept in the spare room, which he did quite often. Dylan had woken me up – early, as usual – and was chattering away at me. I got him out of his cot and went downstairs. Ordinarily, I would have put him in the living room and gone into the kitchen to make breakfast, but for some reason on this day, I went into the living room first. We had this tiny little coffee table, and on it were all these drugs and a rolled-up bank note.

Dylan was walking by this point and it's horrific to think what could have happened. I was so angry that I called the police. They came round and looked but said they couldn't do anything. They said they could take the drugs away for testing, but there didn't seem much point. It was massively frustrating. What's the point of this stuff being illegal if you can't do anything? I asked them if this amount of drugs could have killed my baby. The policeman said it probably could. He looked at me and said, 'You know what this is, I know what this is, and you've got a two-year-old. Don't be a mug.' And I just thought, 'Yes, you're right, I'm not a mug!'

I rang my parents and told them I was kicking him out. I felt terrible because it was my mum's birthday, but I knew I had to do it there and then. I went into the bedroom and woke him up. I told him by the time I got back, he had to be gone. Then I went to my parents. When I came back, he'd gone.

I had booked an expensive holiday to the hotel where we'd had our honeymoon, for what would have been our third anniversary, around a month later. Being the breadwinner I had paid for it, so I took my friend instead, and I cried the whole time. On our anniversary, he sent me an email saying he was very aware of the date, and he was upset and could we give things another go? But he was obviously out on the piss, so I deleted it. That was the only time he ever tried. Within a couple of months, he was in a relationship with the woman who became his next wife. And that was it! Within a few months, we were properly divorced. I just needed it sorted and done.

He was quite consistent with Dylan when he was little, and Dylan loved his fun dad. Everyone used to say to me, 'Don't worry, one day he'll realise he's an absolute idiot', but I never wanted that. I wanted him to be consistent and stable, and for them to be close. I didn't want to hurt my kid. But over the years, it's been hit-and-miss. My now ex-husband has an addiction problem and he's very unreliable. If he commits to something, there's a good chance he won't turn up and do it. He's gone on benders, just disappeared, and there have been chunks of time when we haven't seen him. The last one lasted nearly a year.

As my career progressed and I built my businesses, I was quite guarded about all this with the people I worked with. I didn't want them to worry that I wouldn't be able to be there for stuff because I had this big responsibility at home. Then I got asked to do a TEDx talk. I had about a year before the talk to prepare for it. I was working with this woman on my plans, and I was going to do it on a work-related topic that was relatively safe and non-controversial. She asked me to talk about where my grit comes from. I ended up telling her my story and she encouraged me to talk about it publicly. Once I did, I started getting messages from people who related to my story. Since then, I've never stopped talking about it – it's a big part of me. There's no point pretending it's not.

Dylan is ten now, and he's really impressive – incredibly smart and artistic. He's at a great school doing amazing things. Recently, there was something on at school and he invited his dad, and then he came to me and said he didn't want him to come because he'd be embarrassing. Sometimes if he's with his dad he'll come back early. He says he feels awkward around him and can't be himself. It's sad, but it's out of my control now. You can't force people to do something: ultimately, you need to have people in your life who share your values. I never let anyone down – as soon as I have committed to doing something, I'll do it – because I've said I would. So I can't understand why he can't come and pick up his kid at the time he said he would. But I've realised I can't control it. He's going to do what he's going to do. I'm civil with him, and if he did a bit more parenting that would be awesome, but he's just not capable of it. I still feel annoyed and frustrated, and we'll never be friends, which is a shame.

I sometimes find myself feeling jealous of women who have got an equal partner. My brother has a senior role as a finance director and his wife is a buyer for a shopping channel. He's so supportive of her – as he should be. I think they support each other well – my perception of their marriage is that they are very equal around how they prioritise things and how they share things. I feel jealous that she can travel for work, and he will juggle the kids and get them to their clubs, handling things at home. I get very resentful because I look at my ex-husband, who decides he doesn't want to do something and doesn't do it. He sees Dylan on Sundays now, but if he gets drunk on Saturday night he just won't show up, and he might not even tell me.

Looking back, I know ending the marriage was the best thing I could have done. Kids are not stupid – if they live in a dysfunctional household, they see that as acceptable and normal. In my view, it's much better for a kid to see both of their parents happy, even if that means they are apart. That's all Dylan has ever known, but I'm pleased he's not watching a relationship play out that is setting all the wrong examples."

It's not just some ex-husbands who are useless – some current husbands are useless too! Many men of my generation grew up in very traditional households, with stay-at-home mums and working dads. They haven't necessarily clocked that for women to lead lives different from those of their mothers, they need to break away from the patterns they grew up observing. Their own father may never have done the school run, or cooked dinner, or made the packed lunches. Having said this, many women didn't grow up with professional working mothers showing them how to thrive in both arenas either, but we seem to be doing OK!

Some men are absolutely adapting to these changes – I see lots of men (including my own husband!) who see their partner as an equal and share the running of the household and the family. I also see lots of women who are completely burned out by trying – and, yes, I know it's a cliché – to work as if they have no children and to parent as if they don't work. The so-called mental load of parenting – keeping on top of the laundry, grocery shopping, taking your child to parties, buying gifts for friends and teachers, remembering who likes which vegetables with dinner – it goes on. If you add this to running a business, being a doctor or managing a classful of rowdy kids, it's a huge mental strain. We need partners who can support us and be part of the team, not create more work for us.

What Rebecca's story shows me is the sheer strength and brilliance of women. To raise a happy child as a single mother, achieve the sort of professional success she has, and be a great person too. I find it inspiring. What I hope is that the next generation of boys will grow up in this new reality and will be kind, supportive, responsible partners who see being a hands-on dad and supportive partner as the norm, not an exception.

But for this to happen, we need to support boys and young men to find a new place in the world. We need to remove the negativity around men and help them through this difficult time in our social development. We need them to grow up with pride and honour and allow them to be brilliant men, rather than shouting them down. Yes, we need men to come to the table – and when they do, we need to let them, and allow them to express their masculinity in a positive way.

Chapter Twenty-Three
Be part of the support crew

Louise is a fifty-two-year-old mum of two sons, aged twenty-four and eighteen. She lives in Buckinghamshire with her husband of thirty years and has worked in health and social care for twenty years.

I met my husband-to-be when I was twenty-one. I wasn't looking for love but we instantly connected. Richard is kind, generous and loyal: we found we shared the same sense of humour and zest for life – we were party animals and carefree. I had no idea what I was going to do career wise, and I jumped around between jobs, feeling uninspired. We travelled a lot and had a large group of friends, never taking life too seriously.

We married when I was twenty-five (Richard is eleven years older than me) and agreed that, at some point, we would like to have children. I had a real mix of friends, some who were like minded but struggling to find a life partner, and others who were settled and resolute that children were not for them.

I had our first child, Charlie, when I was twenty-seven. He was three months premature and weighed just 2 lb 13 oz. Over the next few weeks, we were hit with wave after wave of bad news, often delivered with great insensitivity – 'Your son has a chromosomal abnormality. Do you know what that means?' Well, it meant he had Down's syndrome, but they didn't tell us that it was a very rare form until we pressed them to explain what 'translocation' meant on his notes. He had a cleft palate, a hole in his heart, chronic lung disease and was likely to be suffering from brain damage. It was one devastating diagnosis after another. Charlie was so unwell that he stopped breathing a couple of times, and they brought him back. I recall standing there, watching doctors and nurses working on him in front of me, and I was incapable of doing anything. It was an incredibly shocking and difficult time. My mother has always said that it made me grow up overnight: I literally changed from one person to another. While I was grieving and shocked, our sole focus become Charlie's survival.

Charlie was in hospital for seventeen weeks. He came home on oxygen and with a feeding tube, and my home became an extension of a special care baby unit. Far from relishing finally having my baby home, I realised that I was very isolated. In hospital, we had the nurses to chat with and other parents to share the ups and downs with, but now I was on my own at home. Richard had to return to work.

My friendships changed. A lot of people just didn't know what to say. I found myself breaking the news about Charlie and his diagnosis in the gentlest way possible, because I had to cope with the reactions. If the response to the news was bad, the person distressed and uncomfortable, with a whirlwind of platitudes and pity, I couldn't cope with it. I found (and it's still the case today) that I didn't like it when people said to me, 'Oh, but people with Down's are so loving, aren't they?' I know it comes from a good place but Down's is much more complicated than that – and it doesn't negate the feelings of utter despair that so many people feel when they have a child who will need care for the rest of their life.

The number of friends in our lives reduced to a third of what it had been. We were not the party people anymore. I say this with no criticism or judgement. It was a complicated situation that not everyone is cut out for, and I was still only in my late twenties.

Our lives became much smaller and more concentrated. It really was the two of us against the world. I had one very good friend, who would turn up for a weekend, clean the house, go with Richard to do the week's food shopping and give me a cuddle. She was a lifeline and always there for me. She still is. I honestly don't know what I would have done without her.

When Charlie was about eighteen months old and starting to stabilise, I had a breakdown. Suddenly it all hit me: all the stuff I had pushed down so I could weather the storm had taken its toll. I never saw it coming. I was twenty-nine, and it was like a tsunami. It threw everything up in the air.

After a consultation with the GP, I was prescribed antidepressants. Even today, there seems to still be some stigma about taking this type of medication. I felt that taking them, in conjunction with counselling, was the right thing to do, and it certainly worked for me. It's like learning to ride a bike again: you may need some stabilisers, and that's what the antidepressants were for me. But I knew I needed to address the deeper issues too, otherwise I was never going to function properly again.

I started weekly counselling. Each time I went, I remember parking, walking down the path to reception, thinking, 'Well, this is just ridiculous. It's probably a massive waste of my time.' And then I got in there, and after about five minutes everything flooded out of me, and I was in tears. It was a safe place where I could say whatever I needed to without fear of judgement. I could explore my feelings with support. I know that I said things in those sessions that I have never repeated anywhere else – it was intensely private.

I was finally having to deal with my overwhelming feelings of sadness. I was grieving for Charlie, for the life I thought he was going to have but now absolutely wasn't. I was grieving for me, for my husband, for the life we imagined we were going to have. I was terrified about what Charlie's life would be like, because I knew I wouldn't live forever. Who was going to protect him? Where would he live? And there was still so much to come, so many surgeries.

As Charlie moved through childhood, we couldn't go out socially very much. Charlie was not a good sleeper so if we did have a late night, we really paid for it. We encouraged people to come to us, as home was an environment we could control, to a certain extent.

Knowing that Charlie had been diagnosed with a rare form of Down's syndrome had implications for both him and us. For Richard and me, it meant we may be carriers – so, every time we conceive, there is a very high chance that the baby will have Down's. We had to have genetic testing. I had already decided that everything that happened with Charlie – his premature birth, all his defects and diagnosis – was my fault. Therefore, I decreed that there would be no more children. The genetic testing informed us that Charlie was a one-off – we were not carriers. Richard very gently, patiently and lovingly worked on me for six years until I finally gave in, and we had our second son, Harry. I am pleased to say that he is a fabulous, healthy human, but I take nothing for granted. I often worry that something will happen to him, which I think harks back to my very early grief and worry. While I have learned to live with it, it will never leave me.

Charlie has a very high chance of developing Alzheimer's as he grows older, and that is what took me into a career in care. I applied for a job working for a care home company in sales and marketing. Over time, I was encouraged to move into more operational roles, eventually running a dementia unit. I finally discovered that I had 'found my home'... and my calling.

As my career took off when I was in my mid-thirties, Richard, who was self-employed and able to be more flexible, took a back seat. He encouraged me to be the breadwinner and he made sure the ship stayed afloat at home. At first, it was harder than he realised. He felt conflicted as our roles were swapped. While there is less stigma about stay-at-home dads these days, there was quite a bit then. I'm not sure what his family made of it; I'm not sure they ever understood. He was, and is to this day, a great dad. He had a mix of madness and a wacky sense of humour: his boys love him enormously and he is their greatest champion.

Perhaps what we didn't foresee initially was how my world would suddenly open up again, whereas Richard's world shrank and his contact with others became very limited. When we realised what was happening, Richard built new networks for himself, but it took time. Meanwhile, my life comprised working ridiculously long hours, including commuting into London and catching up with jobs around the home at weekends. I was often exhausted. I wasn't seeing friends – I was certainly not investing in friendships.

Everyone has a story about how the pandemic was for them; some are more positive than others. Work was changing for me, and I was no longer with the same colleagues. I realised I needed to invest in friendships again. I felt lonely. My children were getting older and less reliant on me. Richard had an established friendship group and social circle of his own. I realised that I needed to reconnect with girlfriends and say yes more.

There is power in being able to spend time with women you feel a connection with. Whether we talk about shared experiences or individual trials, I find it nurturing. I enjoyed being there for friends, in good times or bad. I didn't realise it at the time, but I had joined a tribe of women who would become amazing friends.

This year has presented me with challenges again. Early in the year, I lost my job. While I was very rational about it and understood the business circumstances that resulted in this outcome, the feelings of worthlessness, low self-esteem and a lack of identity caught me unawares.

But my 'tribe' has continued to help me through it... by giving me great HR advice, introductions to recruiters, and words of encouragement and coaching. Texts and calls checking in, invitations for lunch or bringing dinner over. It's lovely. I feel very honoured by it all. It's also helped me so much. I know I am resilient enough to surf this one, and I know I'll be able to get through it with my women around me.

I believe we have to find more opportunities to build our female networks. Recently, I was at a big awards event. They can be very mixed in terms of enjoyment. However, I found myself at a table full of women, and we had the most fantastic conversation. I don't think I've ever enjoyed an awards lunch as much as I did that one. We found that we had lots of connections, we talked about our dogs, the menopause, the struggles and the juggles of working life, our families, dementia. The next day we set up a group on LinkedIn, and a few weeks later we all got together, inviting other women in leadership roles to join in. Women supporting women is such a powerful thing.

One of my 'tribe' shared this message recently on our WhatsApp group after a fun evening together: 'Feeling lots of gratitude and full up after our time together. Friendship really is the best medicine. Thank you, ladies, you are the best.'

I think that says it all."

We all know what our biological response to stress is: fight-or-flight. The term was first coined in 1915 and has been researched time and time again, but before the 1990s women only made up about 17 per cent of participants in studies of the stress response.

A fascinating piece of work in 2006[1] turned the fight-or-flight narrative on its head. That's not necessarily what women do. Dr Shelley Taylor and her team coined a term, 'tend and befriend', to describe what, until then, had been unexplored – the female stress regulatory system. If you think about it, it makes perfect sense. Our response to stress has evolved to protect ourselves and our children. If we were to fight a predator, we would be unlikely to win. We are also less likely than a man to outrun a threat – do you know a woman who, in the face of a threat, would run away and leave her babies behind?

'Tend and befriend' makes perfect sense to me. Tending involves nurturing and taking care of those around us – behaviour designed to protect ourselves and our offspring from the stressful situation, and to reduce distress. It is being close to the people we love. Befriending is reaching out for social networks that promote feelings of connection and safety. Understanding that this is what we need when we are under stress means we can capitalise on this natural response and make the most of it.

We can't all be friends. No group can be expected to get along just because they have biology in common. That would be ludicrous – and patronising.

But find your people and lean on them. Be there for your women. Recognise when they need help – they might not realise it themselves. Make time for your village. If you have to, diarise it. Reach out, even if it's been a while. It doesn't matter who reaches out first, as long as someone does. I recently heard a *Woman's Hour* episode that said women find it harder to reach out to an old friend than to make a new one. While it was still playing, I WhatsApped one of my friends, who I deeply regretted losing touch with a couple of years before. I'm so happy to have her back in my life, and I will never let her go again!

We need our women and they need us. Let's form a new kind of village – a new kitchen table – and support each other on this crazy journey through life.

---

1. *Current Directions in Psychological Science*: (Journal, 2006) Tend and befriend: biobehavioral bases of affiliation under stress.

Chapter Twenty-Four

The next generation

Amelia is thirteen. She is Louise's daughter – and the inspiration for this book. She is at senior (secondary) school, and lives with her parents and brother Rudy in Hampshire. She enjoys horse riding and spending time with her friends.

"I'm just about to finish Year 8 at senior school. It's been a difficult couple of years. While I've made some really good friends, I haven't enjoyed it there. I went to a small primary school and the senior school is big, with almost 2,000 kids – there are 400 in my year alone. It's quite a daunting place to go. I want to learn, and I want to do well at school, but because the school is so big, I've felt a bit lost. It's hard to learn because there are too many people, and lots of naughty kids that get all the attention. I don't get much help when I need it and I don't feel like I'm learning as much as I could.

A few months ago, one of my friends left to go to a different school – a much smaller school with a good reputation. It made me and my parents think that maybe I could move too. When we went to look around, it felt really homely. It didn't feel like a big block building; it was welcoming. I spent two taster days there and, even though I felt nervous, found the lessons more engaging, and I felt like I knew what I was doing. I didn't feel like it was just about getting through it; it felt worthwhile. So we decided I would move.

I leave my current school in two days' time. I'm looking forward to moving but I'm sad to be leaving my friends. Some of them I've known since I was four! It's a bit scary to be in a new environment with people you don't know and to make new friends. I think it will be more like the junior school I went to – smaller and more friendly, and I'll get to know all the teachers. I hope I'll find a good friendship group and enjoy the lessons. It's also the first time I'll have to take a bus by myself, and I'm nervous about that, but I know what I need to do and I know it will be OK once I've done it a few times.

I'm excited about going to the new school because I think it will give me more opportunities to do well in my exams, get into college and do what I want in life. I don't know what I want to do yet, but I believe this will give me more options."

Amelia is so much stronger than I was at her age. She's more mature, too. I don't know whether it's nature or nurture, but she seems to be able to think through challenges in her life so clearly. I'm lucky that she has always been able, and willing, to talk to me in detail about her life, her thoughts and her feelings. I'm always amazed by how coherent and articulate she is about what – even to some adults – would be big emotions. My husband Paul and I find space and time to have conversations with her as an adult, encouraging her to be honest with herself, and us, about how she feels. This generation of girls seems more able to do that than previous generations, and I think they are encouraged more to do it, too.

Don't get me wrong, it's not all roses in our house; raising strong girls is tough. Sometimes, when Amelia is shouting at me because she disagrees with my parenting choices, I wonder whether raising her to be a strong, independent, feisty girl was a good idea after all! But I know it will stand her in good stead. Nobody will ever take advantage of her, that's for sure!

She spends hours talking to her friends on the phone, and sometimes I listen to them, hopeful that this is the start of her building those female bonds that will nurture and protect her through her life. Some of her closest friends are not from school, but people she has met through her hobbies. She gravitates to people who share her values and interests and doesn't seem at all worried about being popular. I make sure she knows how important my female friendships are to me and try to help her nurture her own.

My son, Rudy, is so different. He's full of energy and fun. He's funny and sporty, confident and popular at school. He's loving and cuddly, but he holds his feelings in. I worry about him more than I do about Amelia. I worry about where our boys will find themselves in ten years' time. We need boys and men to step into this brave new world with us, but we also need to make sure they have a place in it: a place that celebrates and appreciates all the best things about men and dials down the narrative about toxic masculinity. In our fight to improve the lives of women, we must make sure we don't make every man our enemy but find a way to work together.

The next generation has a scary time ahead. Whether it's war or climate change, the world seems to be getting more confusing by the day. I hope we can prepare our children for it, by sharing with them as much wisdom as we can and acknowledging that they will learn their own lessons. Maybe they'll even teach us some things, if we stay open-minded enough to listen to them!

Epilogue

What next?

Thank you for joining me at my newly created kitchen table and listening to the stories of the amazing women who have so generously shared such personal parts of themselves, so we can learn and be inspired by their experiences.

Of you, the reader, I ask three things:

1: Create your own kitchen table

When I first started Project Sunlight, I asked women to talk to me about their lives, their experiences, and the stories that had shaped them. Almost every single woman I asked said they didn't know if they had anything interesting to talk about. Some thought they couldn't share because they still haven't dealt with the things that happened to them. Some even said they thought their lives were unremarkable and boring. As we can see from their stories, and the many others I heard but couldn't share in this book, every woman has wisdom to share.

The other impact these stories had is with the women themselves. After the interview with each woman, I wrote the story up and sent it back to her to review, to make sure she was happy with how it was represented. Some of the women had strong reactions to seeing their own stories written down – they told me they felt validated, or that it reframed something for them. Thinking about our own stories deeply enough to share them with someone else can be a very powerful thing to do.

Every story is powerful. Ask the women in your life about themselves. Their work. Their community. Ask them what they think about the world, and why. Tell your own stories wherever you can. You never know who you might be helping.

2: Read, learn, and share

At the end of this book, I have included a QR code to a list of references, suggested further reading and other resources relevant to the themes in this book. Unless we educate ourselves and each other on some of these issues, we're not going to change them. Read the reports. Explore the books and recommend them to others. Explore whether there is an organisation or charity that can support you, or that you could support. Talk about the things you've learned. Quote the statistics. Share the knowledge.

If you feel that you need support after reading these stories, please reach out for help.

3: Join our community

When I started Project Sunlight, I had no idea where it was going. There were times over the two years when I thought it was crazy, and I put it down for weeks at a time. But I kept coming back to it because it felt important. The women I was talking to were enriching my life, and their stories were inspiring me so directly that I was drawing on them at difficult times and talking about them to other people. My hope is that Project Sunlight might become a place where women can gather and raise their voices, so that we might all benefit.

Please join us.

Resources

Scan the QR code below to access the resources referenced throughout Her Voice, further reading, and support organisations.

Acknowledgements

To all the women who gave me their time and opened their hearts to share their stories, thank you. Project Sunlight has changed my life and I will be forever grateful.

To my women – my mum, grandma, step mum, and incredible network of friends and colleagues, thank you. My world is infinitely better with you in it.

To my beautiful children who inspire me every day to be a better person. Thank you.

To my husband, Paul, who listened to me talk incessantly about Project Sunlight, gave me the idea to tell stories, and has supported me throughout this experience and everything else in our lives. Thank you.

About the author

Louise Atkinson is a passionate advocate of women supporting women, believing in the power of shared purpose and connection. She devotes much of her time to supporting and cultivating communities, creating safe spaces for women to be honest, vulnerable and real.

For the last two years, Louise has worked to harness the magic of these communities driven by one vision – *every woman has an incredible story to tell*. Stories that may seem commonplace and unremarkable on the surface; Louise has flipped the narrative to demonstrate that these everyday stories are what make all women extraordinary.

Louise launched Project Sunlight in 2022 – working with women from all walks of life to tell their stories, in their own words. Project Sunlight was created to celebrate these women and support others to share their own stories. It serves as the inspiration behind *Her Voice*.

Louise has spent most of her professional life working in large, corporate, male-dominated organisations and is currently a senior leader in the defence industry. She regularly speaks at industry-leading events and is a mentor to women inside and outside of work. She is proud mum of two, and lives with her family in Hampshire.